The Poetry of Algernon Charles Swinburne

VOLUME XI – A DARK MONTH & OTHER POEMS

Algernon Charles Swinburne was born on April 5th, 1837, in London, into a wealthy Northumbrian family. He was educated at Eton and at Balliol College, Oxford, but did not complete a degree.

In 1860 Swinburne published two verse dramas but achieved his first literary success in 1865 with Atalanta in Calydon, written in the form of classical Greek tragedy. The following year "Poems and Ballads" brought him instant notoriety. He was now identified with "indecent" themes and the precept of art for art's sake.

Although he produced much after this success in general his popularity and critical reputation declined. The most important qualities of Swinburne's work are an intense lyricism, his intricately extended and evocative imagery, metrical virtuosity, rich use of assonance and alliteration, and bold, complex rhythms.

Swinburne's physical appearance was small, frail, and plagued by several other oddities of physique and temperament. Throughout the 1860s and 1870s he drank excessively and was prone to accidents that often left him bruised, bloody, or unconscious. Until his forties he suffered intermittent physical collapses that necessitated removal to his parents' home while he recovered.

Throughout his career Swinburne also published literary criticism of great worth. His deep knowledge of world literatures contributed to a critical style rich in quotation, allusion, and comparison. He is particularly noted for discerning studies of Elizabethan dramatists and of many English and French poets and novelists. As well he was a noted essayist and wrote two novels.

In 1879, Swinburne's friend and literary agent, Theodore Watts-Dunton, intervened during a time when Swinburne was dangerously ill. Watts-Dunton isolated Swinburne at a suburban home in Putney and gradually weaned him from alcohol, former companions and many other habits as well.

Much of his poetry in this period may be inferior but some individual poems are exceptional; "By the North Sea," "Evening on the Broads," "A Nympholept," "The Lake of Gaube," and "Neap-Tide."

Swinburne lived another thirty years with Watts-Dunton. He denied Swinburne's friends access to him, controlled the poet's money, and restricted his activities. It is often quoted that 'he saved the man but killed the poet'.

Swinburne died on April 10th, 1909 at the age of seventy-two.

Index of Contents

Sonnets:
Hope and Fear
After Sunset
A Study From Memory
To Dr. John Brown
To William Bell Scott
A Death on Easter Day
On the Deaths of Thomas Carlyle and George Eliot
After Looking into Carlyle's Reminiscences
A Last Look
Dickens
On Lamb's Specimens of Dramatic Poets
To John Nichol
Dysthanatos
Euonymos
On the Russian Persecution of the Jews
Bismarck at Canossa
Quia Nominor Leo
The Channel Tunnel
Sir William Gomm
Euthanatos
First and Last
Lines on the Death of Edward John Trelawny
Adieux à Marie Stuart
Herse
Twins
The Salt of the Earth
Seven Years Old
Eight Years Old
Comparisons
What is Death?
A Child's Pity
A Child's Laughter
A Child's Thanks
A Child's Battles
A Child's Future
Sonnets on English Dramatic Poets (1590-1650):
Christopher Marlowe
William Shakespeare
Ben Jonson
Beaumont and Fletcher
Philip Massinger
John Ford
John Webster
Thomas Decker
Thomas Middleton
Thomas Heywood
George Chapman

A DARK MONTH

'La maison sans enfants!'—VICTOR HUGO.

I.

A month without sight of the sun
Rising or reigning or setting
Through days without use of the day,
Who calls it the month of May?
The sense of the name is undone
And the sound of it fit for forgetting.
We shall not feel if the sun rise,
We shall not care when it sets:
If a nightingale make night's air
As noontide, why should we care?
Till a light of delight that is done rise,
Extinguishing grey regrets;

Till a child's face lighten again
On the twilight of older faces;
Till a child's voice fall as the dew
On furrows with heat parched through
And all but hopeless of grain,
Refreshing the desolate places—

Fall clear on the ears of us hearkening
And hungering for food of the sound
And thirsting for joy of his voice:
Till the hearts in us hear and rejoice,
And the thoughts of them doubting and darkening
Rejoice with a glad thing found.

When the heart of our gladness is gone,

What comfort is left with us after?
When the light of our eyes is away,
What glory remains upon May,
What blessing of song is thereon
If we drink not the light of his laughter?

No small sweet face with the daytime
To welcome, warmer than noon!
No sweet small voice as a bird's
To bring us the day's first words!
Mid May for us here is not Maytime!
No summer begins with June.

A whole dead month in the dark,
A dawn in the mists that o'ercome her
Stifled and smothered and sad—
Swift speed to it, barren and bad!
And return to us, voice of the lark,
And remain with us, sunlight of summer.

II.

Alas, what right has the dawn to glimmer,
What right has the wind to do aught but moan?
All the day should be dimmer
Because we are left alone.

Yestermorn like a sunbeam present
Hither and thither a light step smiled,
And made each place for us pleasant
With the sense or the sight of a child.

But the leaves persist as before, and after
Our parting the dull day still bears flowers
And songs less bright than his laughter
Deride us from birds in the bowers.

Birds, and blossoms, and sunlight only,
As though such folly sufficed for spring!
As though the house were not lonely
For want of the child its king!

III.

Asleep and afar to-night my darling
Lies, and heeds not the night,

If winds be stirring or storms be snarling;
For his sleep is its own sweet light.

I sit where he sat beside me quaffing
The wine of story and song
Poured forth of immortal cups, and laughing
When mirth in the draught grew strong.

I broke the gold of the words, to melt it
For hands but seven years old,
And they caught the tale as a bird, and felt it
More bright than visible gold.

And he drank down deep, with his eyes broad beaming,
Here in this room where I am,
The golden vintage of Shakespeare, gleaming
In the silver vessels of Lamb.

Here by my hearth where he was I listen
For the shade of the sound of a word,
Athirst for the birdlike eyes to glisten,
For the tongue to chirp like a bird.

At the blast of battle, how broad they brightened,
Like fire in the spheres of stars,
And clung to the pictured page, and lightened
As keen as the heart of Mars!

At the touch of laughter, how swift it twittered
The shrillest music on earth;
How the lithe limbs laughed and the whole child glittered
With radiant riot of mirth!

Our Shakespeare now, as a man dumb-stricken,
Stands silent there on the shelf:
And my thoughts, that had song in the heart of them, sicken,
And relish not Shakespeare's self.

And my mood grows moodier than Hamlet's even,
And man delights not me,
But only the face that morn and even
My heart leapt only to see.

That my heart made merry within me seeing,
And sang as his laugh kept time:
But song finds now no pleasure in being,
And love no reason in rhyme.

IV.

Mild May-blossom and proud sweet bay-flower,
What, for shame, would you have with us here?
It is not the month of the May-flower
This, but the fall of the year.

Flowers open only their lips in derision,
Leaves are as fingers that point in scorn:
The shows we see are a vision;
Spring is not verily born.

Yet boughs turn supple and buds grow sappy,
As though the sun were indeed the sun:
And all our woods are happy
With all their birds save one.

But spring is over, but summer is over,
But autumn is over, and winter stands
With his feet sunk deep in the clover
And cowslips cold in his hands.

His hoar grim head has a hawthorn bonnet,
His gnarled gaunt hand has a gay green staff
With new-blown rose-blossom on it:
But his laugh is a dead man's laugh.

The laugh of spring that the heart seeks after,
The hand that the whole world yearns to kiss,
It rings not here in his laughter,
The sign of it is not this.

There is not strength in it left to splinter
Tall oaks, nor frost in his breath to sting:
Yet it is but a breath as of winter,
And it is not the hand of spring.

V.

Thirty-one pale maidens, clad
All in mourning dresses,
Pass, with lips and eyes more sad
That it seems they should be glad,
Heads discrowned of crowns they had,
Grey for golden tresses.

Grey their girdles too for green,
And their veils dishevelled:
None would say, to see their mien,
That the least of these had been
Born no baser than a queen,
Reared where flower-fays revelled.

Dreams that strive to seem awake,
Ghosts that walk by daytime,
Weary winds the way they take,
Since, for one child's absent sake,
May knows well, whate'er things make
Sport, it is not Maytime.

VI.

A hand at the door taps light
As the hand of my heart's delight:
It is but a full-grown hand,
Yet the stroke of it seems to start
Hope like a bird in my heart,
Too feeble to soar or to stand.

To start light hope from her cover
Is to raise but a kite for a plover
If her wings be not fledged to soar.
Desire, but in dreams, cannot ope
The door that was shut upon hope
When love went out at the door.

Well were it if vision could keep
The lids of desire as in sleep
Fast locked, and over his eyes
A dream with the dark soft key
In her hand might hover, and be
Their keeper till morning rise;

The morning that brings after many
Days fled with no light upon any
The small face back which is gone;
When the loved little hands once more
Shall struggle and strain at the door
They beat their summons upon.

VII.

If a soul for but seven days were cast out of heaven and its mirth,
They would seem to her fears like as seventy years upon earth.

Even and morrow should seem to her sorrow as long
As the passage of numberless ages in slumberless song.

Dawn, roused by the lark, would be surely as dark in her sight
As her measureless measure of shadowless pleasure was bright.

Noon, gilt but with glory of gold, would be hoary and grey
In her eyes that had gazed on the depths, unamazed with the day.

Night hardly would seem to make darker her dream never done,
When it could but withhold what a man may behold of the sun.

For dreams would perplex, were the days that should vex her but seven,
The sight of her vision, made dark with division from heaven.

Till the light on my lonely way lighten that only now gleams,
I too am divided from heaven and derided of dreams.

VIII.

A twilight fire-fly may suggest
How flames the fire that feeds the sun:
'A crooked figure may attest
In little space a million.'

But this faint-figured verse, that dresses
With flowers the bones of one bare month,
Of all it would say scarce expresses
In crooked ways a millionth.

A fire-fly tenders to the father
Of fires a tribute something worth:
My verse, a shard-borne beetle rather,
Drones over scarce-illumined earth.

Some inches round me though it brighten
With light of music-making thought,
The dark indeed it may not lighten,
The silence moves not, hearing nought.

Only my heart is eased with hearing,
Only mine eyes are soothed with seeing,
A face brought nigh, a footfall nearing,
Till hopes take form and dreams have being.

IX.

As a poor man hungering stands with insatiate eyes and hands
Void of bread
Right in sight of men that feast while his famine with no least
Crumb is fed,

Here across the garden-wall can I hear strange children call,
Watch them play,
From the windowed seat above, whence the goodlier child I love
Is away.

Here the sights we saw together moved his fancy like a feather
To and fro,
Now to wonder, and thereafter to the sunny storm of laughter
Loud and low—

Sights engraven on storied pages where man's tale of seven swift ages
All was told—
Seen of eyes yet bright from heaven for the lips that laughed were seven
Sweet years old.

X.

Why should May remember
March, if March forget
The days that began with December,
The nights that a frost could fret?

All their griefs are done with
Now the bright months bless
Fit souls to rejoice in the sun with,
Fit heads for the wind's caress;

Souls of children quickening
With the whole world's mirth,
Heads closelier than field-flowers thickening
That crowd and illuminate earth,

Now that May's call musters
Files of baby bands
To marshal in joyfuller clusters
Than the flowers that encumber their hands,

Yet morose November

Found them no less gay,
With nought to forget or remember
Less bright than a branch of may.

All the seasons moving
Move their minds alike
Applauding, acclaiming, approving
All hours of the year that strike.

So my heart may fret not,
Wondering if my friend
Remember me not or forget not
Or ever the month find end.

Not that love sows lighter
Seed in children sown,
But that life being lit in them brighter
Moves fleeter than even our own.

May nor yet September
Binds their hearts, that yet
Remember, forget, and remember,
Forget, and recall, and forget

XI.

As light on a lake's face moving
Between a cloud and a cloud
Till night reclaim it, reproving
The heart that exults too loud,

The heart that watching rejoices
When soft it swims into sight
Applauded of all the voices
And stars of the windy night,

So brief and unsure, but sweeter
Than ever a moondawn smiled,
Moves, measured of no tune's metre,
The song in the soul of a child;

The song that the sweet soul singing
Half listens, and hardly hears,
Though sweeter than joy-bells ringing
And brighter than joy's own tears;

The song that remembrance of pleasure

Begins, and forgetfulness ends
With a soft swift change in the measure
That rings in remembrance of friends

As the moon on the lake's face flashes,
So haply may gleam at whiles
A dream through the dear deep lashes
Whereunder a child's eye smiles,

And the least of us all that love him
May take for a moment part
With angels around and above him,
And I find place in his heart

XII.

Child, were you kinless and lonely—
Dear, were you kin to me—
My love were compassionate only
Or such as it needs would be.

But eyes of father and mother
Like sunlight shed on you shine:
What need you have heed of another
Such new strange love as is mine?

It is not meet if unruly
Hands take of the children's bread
And cast it to dogs; but truly
The dogs after all would be fed.

On crumbs from the children's table
That crumble, dropped from above,
Mr heart feeds, fed with unstable
Loose waifs of a child's light love.

Though love in your heart were brittle
As glass that breaks with a touch,
You haply would lend him a little
Who surely would give you much.

XIII.

Here is a rough
Rude sketch of my friend,
Faint-coloured enough

And unworthily penned.

Fearlessly fair
And triumphant he stands,
And holds unaware
Friends' hearts in his hands;

Stalwart and straight
As an oak that should bring
Forth gallant and great
Fresh roses in spring.

On the paths of his pleasure
All graces that wait
What metre shall measure
What rhyme shall relate

Each action, each motion,
Each feature, each limb,
Demands a devotion
In honour of him:

Head that the hand
Of a god might have blest,
Laid lustrous and bland
On the curve of its crest:

Mouth sweeter than cherries
Keen eyes as of Mars
Browner than berries
And brighter than stars.

Nor colour nor wordy
Weak song can declare
The stature how sturdy,
How stalwart his air.

As a king in his bright
Presence-chamber may be,
So seems he in height—
Twice higher than your knee.

As a warrior sedate
With reserve of his power,
So seems he in state—
As tall as a flower:

As a rose overtowering

The ranks of the rest
That beneath it lie cowering,
Less bright than their best

And his hands are as sunny
As ruddy ripe corn
Or the browner-hued honey
From heather-bells borne.

When summer sits proudest,
Fulfilled with its mirth,
And rapture is loudest
In air and on earth,

The suns of all hours
That have ripened the roots
Bring forth not such flowers
And beget not such fruits.

And well though I know it,
As fain would I write,
Child, never a poet
Could praise you aright.

I bless you? the blessing
Were less than a jest
Too poor for expressing;
I come to be blest,

With humble and dutiful
Heart, from above:
Bless me, O my beautiful
Innocent love!

This rhyme in your praise
With a smile was begun;
But the goal of his ways
Is uncovered to none,

Nor pervious till after
The limit impend;
It is not in laughter
These rhymes of you end.

XIV

Spring, and fall, and summer, and winter,

Which may Earth love least of them all,
Whose arms embrace as their signs imprint her,
Summer, or winter, or spring, or fall?

The clear-eyed spring with the wood-birds mating,
The rose-red summer with eyes aglow,
The yellow fall with serene eyes waiting,
The wild-eyed winter with hair all snow?

Spring's eyes are soft, but if frosts benumb her
As winter's own will her shrewd breath sting:
Storms may rend the raiment of summer,
And fall grow bitter as harsh-lipped spring.

One sign for summer and winter guides me,
One for spring, and the like for fall:
Whichever from sight of my friend divides me,
That is the worst ill season of all.

XV.

Worse than winter is spring
If I come not to sight of my king:
But then what a spring will it be
When my king takes homage of me!

I send his grace from afar
Homage, as though to a star;
As a shepherd whose flock takes flight
May worship a star by night.

As a flock that a wolf is upon
My songs take flight and are gone:
No heart is in any to sing
Aught but the praise of my king.

Fain would I once and again
Sing deeds and passions of men:
But ever a child's head gleams
Between my work and my dreams.

Between my hand and my eyes
The lines of a small face rise,
And the lines I trace and retrace
Are none but those of the face.

Till the tale of all this flock of days alike
All be done,
Weary days of waiting till the month's hand strike
Thirty-one,
Till the clock's hand of the month break off, and end
With the clock,
Till the last and whitest sheep at last be penned
Of the flock,
I their shepherd keep the count of night and day
With my song,
Though my song be, like this month which once was May,
All too long.

The incarnate sun, a tall strong youth,
On old Greek eyes in sculpture smiled:
But trulier had it given the truth
To shape him like a child.

No face full-grown of all our dearest
So lightens all our darkness, none
Most loved of all our hearts hold nearest
So far outshines the sun,

As when with sly shy smiles that feign
Doubt if the hour be clear, the time
Fit to break off my work again
Or sport of prose or rhyme,

My friend peers in on me with merry
Wise face, and though the sky stay dim
The very light of day, the very
Sun's self comes in with him.

Out of sight,
Out of mind!
Could the light
Prove unkind?

Can the sun
Quite forget

What was done
Ere he set?

Does the moon
When she wanes
Leave no tune
That remains

In the void
Shell of night
Overcloyed
With her light?

Must the shore
At low tide
Feel no more
Hope or pride,

No intense
Joy to be,
In the sense
Of the sea—

In the pulses
Of her shocks
It repulses,
When its rocks

Thrill and ring
As with glee?
Has my king
Cast off me,

Whom no bird
Flying south
Brings one word
From his mouth?

Not the ghost
Of a word
Riding post
Have I heard,

Since the day
When my king
Took away
With him spring,

And the cup
Of each flower
Shrivelled up
That same hour,

With no light
Left behind.
Out of sight,
Out of mind!

XIX.

Because I adore you
And fall
On the knees of my spirit before you—
After all,

You need not insult,
My king,
With neglect, though your spirit exult
In the spring.

Even me, though not worth,
God knows,
One word of you sent me in mirth,
Or one rose

Out of all in your garden
That grow
Where the frost and the wind never harden
Flakes of snow,

Nor ever is rain
At all,
But the roses rejoice to remain
Fair and tall—

The roses of love,
More sweet
Than blossoms that rain from above
Round our feet,

When under high bowers
We pass,
Where the west wind freckles with flowers
All the grass.

But a child's thoughts bear
More bright
Sweet visions by day, and more fair
Dreams by night,

Than summer's whole treasure
Can be:
What am I that his thought should take pleasure,
Then, in me?

I am only my love's
True lover,
With a nestful of songs, like doves
Under cover,

That I bring in my cap
Fresh caught,
To be laid on my small king's lap—
Worth just nought

Yet it haply may hap
That he,
When the mirth in his veins is as sap
In a tree,

Will remember me too
Some day
Ere the transit be thoroughly through
Of this May—

Or perchance, if such grace
May be,
Some night when I dream of his face,
Dream of me.

Or if this be too high
A hope
For me to prefigure in my
Horoscope,

He may dream of the place
Where we
Basked once in the light of his face,
Who now see

Nought brighter, not one
Thing bright,
Than the stars and the moon and the sun,

Day nor night

Day by darkling day,
Overpassing, bears away
Somewhat of the burden of this weary May.

Night by numbered night,
Waning, brings more near in sight
Hope that grows to vision of my heart's delight

Nearer seems to burn
In the dawn's rekindling urn
Flame of fragrant incense, hailing his return.

Louder seems each bird
In the brightening branches heard
Still to speak some ever more delightful word.

All the mists that swim
Round the dawns that grow less dim
Still wax brighter and more bright with hope of him,

All the suns that rise
Bring that day more near our eyes
When the sight of him shall clear our clouded skies.

All the winds that roam
Fruitful fields or fruitless foam
Blow the bright hour near that brings his bright face home,

I hear of two far hence
In a garden met,
And the fragrance blown from thence
Fades not yet.

The one is seven years old,
And my friend is he:
But the years of the other have told
Eighty-three.

To hear these twain converse
Or to see them greet

Were sweeter than softest verse
May be sweet.

The hoar old gardener there
With an eye more mild
Perchance than his mild white hair
Meets the child.

I had rather hear the words
That the twain exchange
Than the songs of all the birds
There that range,

Call, chirp, and twitter there
Through the garden-beds
Where the sun alike sees fair
Those two heads,

And which may holier be
Held in heaven of those
Or more worth heart's thanks to see
No man knows.

XXII.

Of such is the kingdom of heaven.
No glory that ever was shed
From the crowning star of the seven
That crown the north world's head,

No word that ever was spoken
Of human or godlike tongue,
Gave ever such godlike token
Since human harps were strung.

No sign that ever was given
To faithful or faithless eyes
Showed ever beyond clouds riven
So clear a Paradise.

Earth's creeds may be seventy times seven
And blood have denied each creed:
If of such be the kingdom of heaven,
It must be heaven indeed

XXIII.

The wind on the downs is bright
As though from the sea:
And morning and night
Take comfort again with me.

He is nearer to-day,
Each night to each morning saith,
Whose return shall revive dead May
With the balm of his breath.

The sunset says to the moon,
He is nearer to-night
Whose coming in June
Is looked for more than the light.

Bird answers to bird,
Hour passes the sign on to hour,
And for joy of the bright news heard
Flower murmurs to flower.

The ways that were glad of his feet
In the woods that he knew
Grow softer to meet
The sense of his footfall anew.

He is near now as day,
Says hope to the new-born light:
He is near now as June is to May,
Says love to the night.

XXIV.

Good things I keep to console me
For lack of the best of all,
A child to command and control me,
Bid come and remain at his call

Sun, wind, and woodland and highland,
Give all that ever they gave:
But my world is a cultureless island,
My spirit a masterless slave.

And friends are about me, and better
At summons of no man stand:
But I pine for the touch of a fetter,
The curb of a strong king's hand.

Each hour of the day in her season
Is mine to be served as I will:
And for no more exquisite reason
Are all served idly and ill

By slavery my sense is corrupted,
My soul not fit to be free:
I would fain be controlled, interrupted,
Compelled as a thrall may be.

For fault of spur and of bridle
I tire of my stall to death:
My sail flaps joyless and idle
For want of a small child's breath.

XXV.

Whiter and whiter
The dark lines grow,
And broader opens and brighter
The sense of the text below.

Nightfall and morrow
Bring nigher the boy
Whom wanting we want not sorrow,
Whom having we want no joy.

Clearer and clearer
The sweet sense grows
Of the word which hath summer for hearer,
The word on the lips of the rose.

Duskily dwindles
Each deathlike day,
Till June realising rekindles
The depth of the darkness of May.

XXVI.

*"In his bright radiance and collateral light
Must I be comforted, not in his sphere."*

Stars in heaven are many,
Suns in heaven but one:
Nor for man may any

Star supplant the sun.

Many a child as joyous
As our far-off king
Meets as though to annoy us
In the paths of spring.

Sure as spring gives warning,
All things dance in tune:
Sun on Easter morning,
Cloud and windy moon,

Stars between the tossing
Boughs of tuneful trees.
Sails of ships recrossing
Leagues of dancing seas;

Best, in all this playtime,
Best of all in tune,
Girls more glad than Maytime,
Boys more bright than June;

Mixed with all those dances,
Far through field and street
Sing their silent glances,
Ring their radiant feet.

Flowers wherewith May crowned us
Fall ere June be crowned:
Children blossom round us
All the whole year round.

Is the garland worthless
For one rose the less,
And the feast made mirthless?
Love, at least, says yes.

Strange it were, with many
Stars enkindling air,
Should but one find any
Welcome: strange it were,

Had one star alone won
Praise for light from far:
Nay, love needs his own one
Bright particular star,

Hope and recollection

Only lead him right
In its bright reflection
And collateral light.

Find as yet we may not
Comfort in its sphere:
Yet these days will weigh not
When it warms us here;

When full-orbed it rises,
Now divined afar:
None in all the skies is
Half so good a star;

None that seers importune
Till a sign be won:
Star of our good fortune,
Rise and reign, our sun!

XXVII.

I pass by the small room now forlorn
Where once each night as I passed I knew
A child's bright sleep from even to morn
Made sweet the whole night through.

As a soundless shell, as a songless nest,
Seems now the room that was radiant then
And fragrant with his happier rest
Than that of slumbering men.

The day therein is less than the day,
The night is indeed night now therein:
Heavier the dark seems there to weigh,
And slower the dawns begin.

As a nest fulfilled with birds, as a shell
Fulfilled with breath of a god's own hymn,
Again shall be this bare blank cell,
Made sweet again with him.

XXVIII.

Spring darkens before us,
A flame going down,
With chant from the chorus

Of days without crown—
Cloud, rain, and sonorous
Soft wind on the down.

She is wearier not of us
Than we of the dream
That spring was to love us
And joy was to gleam
Through the shadows above us
That shift as they stream.

Half dark and half hoary,
Float far on the loud
Mild wind, as a glory
Half pale and half proud
From the twilight of story,
Her tresses of cloud;

Like phantoms that glimmer
Of glories of old
With ever yet dimmer
Pale circlets of gold
As darkness grows grimmer
And memory more cold.

Like hope growing clearer
With wane of the moon,
Shines toward us the nearer
Gold frontlet of June,
And a face with it dearer
Than midsummer noon.

XXIX.

You send me your love in a letter,
I send you my love in a song:
Ah child, your gift is the better,
Mine does you but wrong.

No fame, were the best less brittle,
No praise, were it wide as earth,
Is worth so much as a little
Child's love may be worth.

We see the children above us
As they might angels above:
Come back to us, child, if you love us,

And bring us your love.

No time for books or for letters:
What time should there be?
No room for tasks and their fetters:
Full room to be free.

The wind and the sun and the Maytirne
Had never a guest
More worthy the most that his playtime
Could give of its best.

If rain should come on, peradventure,
(But sunshine forbid!)
Vain hope in us haply might venture
To dream as it did.

But never may come, of all comers
Least welcome, the rain,
To mix with his servant the summer's
Rose-garlanded train!

He would write, but his hours are as busy
As bees in the sun,
And the jubilant whirl of their dizzy
Dance never is done.

The message is more than a letter,
Let love understand,
And the thought of his joys even better
Than sight of his hand.

Wind, high-souled, full-hearted
South-west wind of the spring!
Ere April and earth had parted,
Skies, bright with thy forward wing,
Grew dark in an hour with the shadow behind it, that bade not a bird dare sing.

Wind whose feet are sunny,
Wind whose wings are cloud,
With lips more sweet than honey
Still, speak they low or loud,

Rejoice now again in the strength of thine heart: let the depth of thy soul wax proud.

We hear thee singing or sighing,
Just not given to sight,
All but visibly flying
Between the clouds and the light,
And the light in our hearts is enkindled, the shadow therein of the clouds put to flight.

From the gift of thine hands we gather
The core of the flowers therein,
Keen glad heart of heather,
Hot sweet heart of whin,
Twin breaths in thy godlike breath close blended of wild spring's wildest of kin.

All but visibly beating
We feel thy wings in the far
Clear waste, and the plumes of them fleeting,
Soft as swan's plumes are,
And strong as a wild swan's pinions, and swift as the flash of the flight of a star.

As the flight of a planet enkindled
Seems thy far soft flight
Now May's reign has dwindled
And the crescent of June takes light
And the presence of summer is here, and the hope of a welcomer presence in sight.

Wind, sweet-souled, great-hearted
Southwest wind on the wold!
From us is a glory departed
That now shall return as of old,
Borne back on thy wings as an eagle's expanding, and crowned with the sundawn's gold.

There is not a flower but rejoices,
There is not a leaf but has heard:
All the fields find voices,
All the woods are stirred:
There is not a nest but is brighter because of the coming of one bright bird.

Out of dawn and morning,
Noon and afternoon,
The sun to the world gives warning
Of news that brightens the moon;
And the stars all night exult with us, hearing of joy that shall come with June.

SUNRISE

If the wind and the sunlight of April and August had mingled the past and hereafter
In a single adorable season whose life were a rapture of love and of laughter,
And the blithest of singers were back with a song; if again from his tomb as from prison,
If again from the night or the twilight of ages Aristophanes had arisen,
With the gold-feathered wings of a bird that were also a god upon earth at his shoulders,
And the gold-flowing laugh of the manhood of old at his lips, for a joy to beholders,
He alone unrebuked of presumption were able to set to some adequate measure
The delight of our eyes in the dawn that restores them the sun of their sense and the pleasure.
For the days of the darkness of spirit are over for all of us here, and the season
When desire was a longing, and absence a thorn, and rejoicing a word without reason.
For the roof overhead of the pines is astir with delight as of jubilant voices,
And the floor underfoot of the bracken and heather alive as a heart that rejoices.
For the house that was childless awhile, and the light of it darkened, the pulse of it dwindled,
Rings radiant again with a child's bright feet, with the light of his face is rekindled.
And the ways of the meadows that knew him, the sweep of the down that the sky's belt closes,
Grow gladder at heart than the soft wind made them whose feet were but fragrant with roses,
Though the fall of the year be upon us, who trusted in June and by June were defrauded,
And the summer that brought us not back the desire of our eyes be gone hence unapplauded.
For July came joyless among us, and August went out from us arid and sterile,
And the hope of our hearts, as it seemed, was no more than a flower that the seasons imperil,
And the joy of our hearts, as it seemed, than a thought which regret had not heart to remember,
Till four dark months overpast were atoned for, and summer began in September.
Hark, April again as a bird in the house with a child's voice hither and thither:
See, May in the garden again with a child's face cheering the woods ere they wither.
June laughs in the light of his eyes, and July on the sunbright cheeks of him slumbers,
And August glows in a smile more sweet than the cadence of gold-mouthed numbers.
In the morning the sight of him brightens the sun, and the noon with delight in him flushes,
And the silence of nightfall is music about him as soft as the sleep that it hushes.
We awake with a sense of a sunrise that is not a gift of the sundawn's giving,
And a voice that salutes us is sweeter than all sounds else in the world of the living,
And a presence that warms us is brighter than all in the world of our visions beholden,
Though the dreams of our sleep were as those that the light of a world without grief makes golden.
For the best that the best of us ever devised as a likeness of heaven and its glory,
What was it of old, or what is it and will be for ever, in song or in story,
Or in shape or in colour of carven or painted resemblance, adored of all ages,
But a vision recorded of children alive in the pictures of old or the pages?
Where children are not, heaven is not, and heaven if they come not again shall be never:
But the face and the voice of a child are assurance of heaven and its promise for ever.

ATHENS:

AN ODE

Ere from under earth again like fire the violet kindle,   [Strophe I.
Ere the holy buds and hoar on olive-branches bloom,
Ere the crescent of the last pale month of winter dwindle,

Shrink, and fall as falls a dead leaf on the dead month's tomb,
Round the hills whose heights the first-born olive-blossom brightened,
Round the city brow-bound once with violets like a bride,
Up from under earth again a light that long since lightened
Breaks, whence all the world took comfort as all time takes pride.
Pride have all men in their fathers that were free before them,
In the warriors that begat us free-born pride have we:
But the fathers of their spirits, how may men adore them,
With what rapture may we praise, who bade our souls be free?
Sons of Athens born in spirit and truth are all born free men;
Most of all, we, nurtured where the north wind holds his reign:
Children all we sea-folk of the Salaminian seamen,
Sons of them that beat back Persia they that beat back Spain.
Since the songs of Greece fell silent, none like ours have risen;
Since the sails of Greece fell slack, no ships have sailed like ours;
How should we lament not, if her spirit sit in prison?
How should we rejoice not, if her wreaths renew their flowers?
All the world is sweeter, if the Athenian violet quicken:
All the world is brighter, if the Athenian sun return:
All things foul on earth wax fainter, by that sun's light stricken:
All ill growths are withered, where those fragrant flower-lights burn.
All the wandering waves of seas with all their warring waters
Roll the record on for ever of the sea-fight there,
When the capes were battle's lists, and all the straits were slaughter's,
And the myriad Medes as foam-flakes on the scattering air.
Ours the lightning was that cleared the north and lit the nations,
But the light that gave the whole world light of old was she:
Ours an age or twain, but hers are endless generations:
All the world is hers at heart, and most of all are we.
Ye that bear the name about you of her glory,   [Antistrophe I.
Men that wear the sign of Greeks upon you sealed,
Yours is yet the choice to write yourselves in story
Sons of them that fought the Marathonian field.
Slaves of no man were ye, said your warrior poet,
Neither subject unto man as underlings:
Yours is now the season here wherein to show it,
If the seed ye be of them that knew not kings.
If ye be not, swords nor words alike found brittle
From the dust of death to raise you shall prevail:
Subject swords and dead men's words may stead you little,
If their old king-hating heart within you fail.
If your spirit of old, and not your bonds, be broken,
If the kingless heart be molten in your breasts,
By what signs and wonders, by what word or token,
Shall ye drive the vultures from your eagles' nests?
All the gains of tyrants Freedom counts for losses;
Nought of all the work done holds she worth the work,
When the slaves whose faith is set on crowns and crosses

Drive the Cossack bear against the tiger Turk.
Neither cross nor crown nor crescent shall ye bow to,
Nought of Araby nor Jewry, priest nor king:
As your watchword was of old, so be it now too:
As from lips long stilled, from yours let healing spring.
Through the fights of old, your battle-cry was healing,
And the Saviour that ye called on was the Sun:
Dawn by dawn behold in heaven your God, revealing
Light from darkness as when Marathon was won.
Gods were yours yet strange to Turk or Galilean,
Light and Wisdom only then as gods adored:
Pallas was your shield, your comforter was Pæan,
From your bright world's navel spake the Sun your Lord.

Though the names be lost, and changed the signs of Light and Wisdom be,   [Epode I.
By these only shall men conquer, by these only be set free:
When the whole world's eye was Athens, these were yours, and theirs were ye.
Light was given you of your wisdom, light ye gave the world again:
As the sun whose godhead lightened on her soul was Hellas then:
Yea, the least of all her children as the chosen of other men.
Change your hearts not with your garments, nor your faith with creeds that change:
Truth was yours, the truth which time and chance transform not nor estrange:
Purer truth nor higher abides not in the reach of time's whole range.
Gods are they in all men's memories and for all time's periods,
They that hurled the host back seaward which had scourged the sea with rods:
Gods for us are all your fathers, even the least of these as gods.
In the dark of days the thought of them is with us, strong to save,
They that had no lord, and made the Great King lesser than a slave;
They that rolled all Asia back on Asia, broken like a wave.
No man's men were they, no master's and no God's but these their own:
Gods not loved in vain nor served amiss, nor all yet overthrown:
Love of country, Freedom, Wisdom, Light, and none save these alone.
King by king came up against them, sire and son, and turned to flee:
Host on host roared westward, mightier each than each, if more might be:
Field to field made answer, clamorous like as wave to wave at sea.
Strife to strife responded, loud as rocks to clangorous rocks respond
Where the deep rings wreck to seamen held in tempest's thrall and bond,
Till when war's bright work was perfect peace as radiant rose beyond:
Peace made bright with fruit of battle, stronger made for storm gone down,
With the flower of song held heavenward for the violet of her crown
Woven about the fragrant forehead of the fostress maiden's town.
Gods arose alive on earth from under stroke of human hands:
As the hands that wrought them, these are dead, and mixed with time's dead sands:
But the godhead of supernal song, though these now stand not, stands.
Pallas is not, Phœbus breathes no more in breathing brass or gold:
Clytæmnestra towers, Cassandra wails, for ever: Time is bold,
But nor heart nor hand hath he to unwrite the scriptures writ of old.
Dead the great chryselephantine God, as dew last evening shed:

Dust of earth or foam of ocean is the symbol of his head:
Earth and ocean shall be shadows when Prometheus shall be dead.

Fame around her warriors living rang through Greece and lightened,   **[Strophe II.**
Moving equal with their stature, stately with their strength:
Thebes and Lacedæmon at their breathing presence brightened,
Sense or sound of them filled all the live land's breadth and length.
All the lesser tribes put on the pure Athenian fashion,
One Hellenic heart was from the mountains to the sea:
Sparta's bitter self grew sweet with high half-human passion,
And her dry thorns flushed aflower in strait Thermopylæ.
Fruitless yet the flowers had fallen, and all the deeds died fruitless,
Save that tongues of after men, the children of her peace,
Took the tale up of her glories, transient else and rootless,
And in ears and hearts of all men left the praise of Greece.
Fair the war-time was when still, as beacon answering beacon,
Sea to land flashed fight, and thundered note of wrath or cheer;
But the strength of noonday night hath power to waste and weaken,
Nor may light be passed from hand to hand of year to year
If the dying deed be saved not, ere it die for ever,
By the hands and lips of men more wise than years are strong;
If the soul of man take heed not that the deed die never,
Clothed about with purple and gold of story, crowned with song.
Still the burning heart of boy and man alike rejoices,
Hearing words which made it seem of old for all who sang
That their heaven of heavens waxed happier when from free men's voices
Well-beloved Harmodius and Aristogeiton rang.
Never fell such fragrance from the flower-month's rose-red kirtle
As from chaplets on the bright friends' brows who slew their lord:
Greener grew the leaf and balmier blew the flower of myrtle
When its blossom sheathed the sheer tyrannicidal sword.
None so glorious garland crowned the feast Panathenæan
As this wreath too frail to fetter fast the Cyprian dove:
None so fiery song sprang sunwards annual as the pæan
Praising perfect love of friends and perfect country's love.

Higher than highest of all those heavens wherefrom the starry   **[Antistrophe II.**
Song of Homer shone above the rolling fight,
Gleams like spring's green bloom on boughs all gaunt and gnarry
Soft live splendour as of flowers of foam in flight,
Glows a glory of mild-winged maidens upward mounting
Sheer through air made shrill with strokes of smooth swift wings
Round the rocks beyond foot's reach, past eyesight's counting,
Up the cleft where iron wind of winter rings
Round a God fast clenched in iron jaws of fetters,
Him who culled for man the fruitful flower of fire,
Bared the darkling scriptures writ in dazzling letters,
Taught the truth of dreams deceiving men's desire,

Gave their water-wandering chariot-seats of ocean
Wings, and bade the rage of war-steeds champ the rein,
Showed the symbols of the wild birds' wheeling motion,
Waged for man's sake war with God and all his train.
Earth, whose name was also Righteousness, a mother
Many-named and single-natured, gave him breath
Whence God's wrath could wring but this word and none other—
He may smite me, yet he shall not do to death.
Him the tongue that sang triumphant while tormented
Sang as loud the sevenfold storm that roared erewhile
Round the towers of Thebes till wrath might rest contented:
Sang the flight from smooth soft-sanded banks of Nile,
When like mateless doves that fly from snare or tether
Came the suppliants landwards trembling as they trod,
And the prayer took wing from all their tongues together—
King of kings, most holy of holies blessed God.
But what mouth may chant again, what heart may know it,
All the rapture that all hearts of men put on
When of Salamis the time-transcending poet
Sang, whose hand had chased the Mede at Marathon?
Darker dawned the song with stormier wings above the watch-fire spread   [Epode II.
Whence from Ida toward the hill of Hermes leapt the light that said
Troy was fallen, a torch funereal for the king's triumphal head.
Dire indeed the birth of Leda's womb that had God's self to sire
Bloomed, a flower of love that stung the soul with fangs that gnaw like fire:
But the twin-born human-fathered sister-flower bore fruit more dire.
Scarce the cry that called on airy heaven and all swift winds on wing,
Wells of river-heads, and countless laugh of waves past reckoning,
Earth which brought forth all, and the orbed sun that looks on everything,
Scarce that cry fills yet men's hearts more full of heart devouring dread
Than the murderous word said mocking, how the child whose blood he shed
Might clasp fast and kiss her father where the dead salute the dead.
But the latter note of anguish from the lips that mocked her lord,
When her son's hand bared against the breast that suckled him his sword,
How might man endure, O Æschylus, to hear it and record?
How might man endure, being mortal yet, O thou most highest, to hear?
How record, being born of woman? Surely not thy Furies near,
Surely this beheld, this only, blasted hearts to death with fear.
Not the hissing hair, nor flakes of blood that oozed from eyes of fire,
Nor the snort of savage sleep that snuffed the hungering heart's desire
Where the hunted prey found hardly space and harbour to respire;
She whose likeness called them—'Sleep ye, ho? what need of you that sleep?'
(Ah, what need indeed, where she was, of all shapes that night may keep
Hidden dark as death and deeper than men's dreams of hell are deep?)
She the murderess of her husband, she the huntress of her son,
More than ye was she, the shadow that no God withstands but one,
Wisdom equal-eyed and stronger and more splendid than the sun.
Yea, no God may stand betwixt us and the shadows of our deeds,

Nor the light of dreams that lighten darkness, nor the prayer that pleads,
But the wisdom equal-souled with heaven, the light alone that leads.
Light whose law bids home those childless children of eternal night,
Soothed and reconciled and mastered and transmuted in men's sight
Who behold their own souls, clothed with darkness once, now clothed with light.
King of kings and father crowned of all our fathers crowned of yore,
Lord of all the lords of song, whose head all heads bow down before,
Glory be to thee from all thy sons in all tongues evermore.

Rose and vine and olive and deep ivy-bloom entwining   **[Strophe III.**
Close the goodliest grave that e'er they closeliest might entwine
Keep the wind from wasting and the sun from too strong shining
Where the sound and light of sweetest songs still float and shine.
Here the music seems to illume the shade, the light to whisper
Song, the flowers to put not odours only forth, but words
Sweeter far than fragrance: here the wandering wreaths twine crisper
Far, and louder far exults the note of all wild birds.
Thoughts that change us, joys that crown and sorrows that enthrone us,
Passions that enrobe us with a clearer air than ours,
Move and breathe as living things beheld round white Colonus,
Audibler than melodies and visibler than flowers.
Love, in fight unconquered, Love, with spoils of great men laden,
Never sang so sweet from throat of woman or of dove:
Love, whose bed by night is in the soft cheeks of a maiden,
And his march is over seas, and low roofs lack not Love;
Nor may one of all that live, ephemeral or eternal,
Fly nor hide from Love; but whoso clasps him fast goes mad.
Never since the first-born year with flowers first-born grew vernal
Such a song made listening hearts of lovers glad or sad.
Never sounded note so radiant at the rayless portal
Opening wide on the all-concealing lowland of the dead
As the music mingling, when her doomsday marked her mortal,
From her own and old men's voices round the bride's way shed,
Round the grave her bride-house, hewn for endless habitation,
Where, shut out from sunshine, with no bridegroom by, she slept;
But beloved of all her dark and fateful generation,
But with all time's tears and praise besprinkled and bewept:
Well-beloved of outcast father and self-slaughtered mother,
Born, yet unpolluted, of their blind incestuous bed;
Best-beloved of him for whose dead sake she died, her brother,
Hallowing by her own life's gift her own born brother's head:

Not with wine or oil nor any less libation   **[Antistrophe III.**
Hallowed, nor made sweet with humbler perfume's breath;
Not with only these redeemed from desecration,
But with blood and spirit of life poured forth to death;
Blood unspotted, spirit unsullied, life devoted,
Sister too supreme to make the bride's hope good,

Daughter too divine as woman to be noted,
Spouse of only death in mateless maidenhood.
Yea, in her was all the prayer fulfilled, the saying
All accomplished—Would that fate would let me wear
Hallowed innocence of words and all deeds, weighing
Well the laws thereof begot on holier air,
Far on high sublimely stablished, whereof only
Heaven is father; nor did birth of mortal mould
Bring them forth, nor shall oblivion lull to lonely
Slumber. Great in these is God, and grows not old.
Therefore even that inner darkness where she perished
Surely seems as holy and lovely, seen aright,
As desirable and as dearly to be cherished,
As the haunt closed in with laurels from the light,
Deep inwound with olive and wild vine inwoven,
Where a godhead known and unknown makes men pale,
But the darkness of the twilight noon is cloven
Still with shrill sweet moan of many a nightingale.
Closer clustering there they make sweet noise together,
Where the fearful gods look gentler than our fear,
And the grove thronged through with birds of holiest feather
Grows nor pale nor dumb with sense of dark things near.
There her father, called upon with signs of wonder,
Passed with tenderest words away by ways unknown,
Not by sea-storm stricken down, nor touched of thunder,
To the dark benign deep underworld, alone.

Third of three that ruled in Athens, kings with sceptral song for staff,   [Epode III.
Gladdest heart that God gave ever milk and wine of thought to quaff,
Clearest eye that lightened ever to the broad lip's lordliest laugh,
Praise be thine as theirs whose tragic brows the loftier leaf engirds
For the live and lyric lightning of thy honey-hearted words,
Soft like sunny dewy wings of clouds and bright as crying of birds;
Full of all sweet rays and notes that make of earth and air and sea
One great light and sound of laughter from one great God's heart, to be
Sign and semblance of the gladness of man's life where men breathe free.
With no Loxian sound obscure God uttered once, and all time heard,
All the soul of Athens, all the soul of England, in that word:
Rome arose the second child of freedom: northward rose the third.
Ere her Boreal dawn came kindling seas afoam and fields of snow,
Yet again, while Europe groaned and grovelled, shone like suns aglow
Doria splendid over Genoa, Venice bright with Dandolo.
Dead was Hellas, but Ausonia by the light of dead men's deeds
Rose and walked awhile alive, though mocked as whom the fen-fire leads
By the creed-wrought faith of faithless souls that mock their doubts with creeds.
Dead are these, and man is risen again: and haply now the Three
Yet coequal and triune may stand in story, marked as free
By the token of the washing of the waters of the sea.

Athens first of all earth's kindred many-tongued and many-kinned
Had the sea to friend and comfort, and for kinsman had the wind:
She that bare Columbus next: then she that made her spoil of Ind.
She that hears not what man's rage but only what the sea-wind saith:
She that turned Spain's ships to cloud-wrack at the blasting of her breath,
By her strengths of strong-souled children and of strong winds done to death.
North and south the Great King's galleons went in Persian wise: and here
She, with Æschylean music on her lips that laughed back fear,
In the face of Time's grey godhead shook the splendour of her spear.
Fair as Athens then with foot upon her foeman's front, and strong
Even as Athens for redemption of the world from sovereign wrong,
Like as Athens crowned she stood before the sun with crowning song.
All the world is theirs with whom is freedom: first of all the free,
Blest are they whom song has crowned and clothed with blessing: these as we,
These alone have part in spirit with the sun that crowns the sea,

April, 1881.

THE STATUE OF VICTOR HUGO

I.

Since in Athens God stood plain for adoration,
Since the sun beheld his likeness reared in stone,
Since the bronze or gold of human consecration
Gave to Greece her guardian's form and feature shown,
Never hand of sculptor, never heart of nation,
Found so glorious aim in all these ages flown
As is theirs who rear for all time's acclamation
Here the likeness of our mightiest and their own.

II.

Theirs and ours and all men's living who behold him
Crowned with garlands multiform and manifold;
Praise and thanksgiving of all mankind enfold him
Who for all men casts abroad his gifts of gold.
With the gods of song have all men's tongues enrolled him,
With the helpful gods have all men's hearts enrolled:
Ours he is who love him, ours whose hearts' hearts hold him
Fast as his the trust that hearts like his may hold.

III.

He, the heart most high, the spirit on earth most blameless,
Takes in charge all spirits, holds all hearts in trust:
As the sea-wind's on the sea his ways are tameless,
As the laws that steer the world his works are just.
All most noble feel him nobler, all most shameless
Feel his wrath and scorn make pale their pride and lust:
All most poor and lowliest, all whose wrongs were nameless,
Feel his word of comfort raise them from the dust

IV.

Pride of place and lust of empire bloody-fruited
Knew the blasting of his breath on leaf and fruit:
Now the hand that smote the death-tree now disrooted
Plants the refuge-tree that has man's hope for root
Ah, but we by whom his darkness was saluted,
How shall now all we that see his day salute?
How should love not seem by love's own speech confuted,
Song before the sovereign singer not be mute?

V.

With what worship, by what blessing, in what measure,
May we sing of him, salute him, or adore,
With what hymn for praise, what thanksgiving for pleasure,
Who had given us more than heaven, and gives us more?
Heaven's whole treasury, filled up full with night's whole treasure,
Holds not so divine or deep a starry store
As the soul supreme that deals forth worlds at leisure
Clothed with light and darkness, dense with flower and ore.

VI.

Song had touched the bourn: fresh verses overflow it,
Loud and radiant, waves on waves on waves that throng;
Still the tide grows, and the sea-mark still below it
Sinks and shifts and rises, changed and swept along.
Rose it like a rock? the waters overthrow it,
And another stands beyond them sheer and strong:
Goal by goal pays down its prize, and yields its poet
Tribute claimed of triumph, palm achieved of song.

VII.

Since his hand that holds the keys of fear and wonder
Opened on the high priest's dreaming eyes a door
Whence the lights of heaven and hell above and under
Shone, and smote the face that men bow down before,
Thrice again one singer's note had cloven in sunder
Night, who blows again not one blast now but four,
And the fourfold heaven is kindled with his thunder,
And the stars about his forehead are fourscore.

VIII.

From the deep soul's depths where alway love abounded
First had risen a song with healing on its wings
Whence the dews of mercy raining balms unbounded
Shed their last compassion even on sceptred things.1
Even on heads that like a curse the crown surrounded
Fell his crowning pity, soft as cleansing springs;
And the sweet last note his wrath relenting sounded
Bade men's hearts be melted not for slaves but kings.

IX.

Next, that faith might strengthen fear and love embolden,
On the creeds of priests a scourge of sunbeams fell:
And its flash made bare the deeps of heaven, beholden
Not of men that cry, Lord, Lord, from church or cell.2
Hope as young as dawn from night obscure and olden
Rose again, such power abides in truth's one spell:
Night, if dawn it be that touches her, grows golden;
Tears, if such as angels weep, extinguish hell.

X.

Through the blind loud mills of barren blear-eyed learning
Where in dust and darkness children's foreheads bow,
While men's labour, vain as wind or water turning
Wheels and sails of dreams, makes life a leafless bough,
Fell the light of scorn and pity touched with yearning,
Next, from words that shone as heaven's own kindling brow.3
Stars were these as watch-fires on the world's waste burning,
Stars that fade not in the fourfold sunrise now.4

XI.

Now the voice that faints not till all wrongs be wroken
Sounds as might the sun's song from the morning's breast,
All the seals of silence sealed of night are broken,
All the winds that bear the fourfold word are blest.
All the keen fierce east flames forth one fiery token;
All the north is loud with life that knows not rest,
All the south with song as though the stars had spoken;
All the judgment-fire of sunset scathes the west.

XII.

Sound of pæan, roll of chanted panegyric,
Though by Pindar's mouth song's trumpet spake forth praise,
March of warrior songs in Pythian mood or Pyrrhic,
Though the blast were blown by lips of ancient days,
Ring not clearer than the clarion of satiric
Song whose breath sweeps bare the plague-infected ways
Till the world be pure as heaven is for the lyric
Sun to rise up clothed with radiant sounds as rays.

XIII.

Clear across the cloud-rack fluctuant and erratic
As the strong star smiles that lets no mourner mourn,
Hymned alike from lips of Lesbian choirs or Attic
Once at evensong and morning newly born,
Clear and sure above the changes of dramatic
Tide and current, soft with love and keen with scorn,
Smiles the strong sweet soul of maidenhood, ecstatic
And inviolate as the red glad mouth of morn.

XIV.

Pure and passionate as dawn, whose apparition
Thrills with fire from heaven the wheels of hours that whirl,
Rose and passed her radiance in serene transition
From his eyes who sought a grain and found a pearl.
But the food by cunning hope for vain fruition
Lightly stolen away from keeping of a churl
Left the bitterness of death and hope's perdition
On the lip that scorn was wont for shame to curl.5

XV.

Over waves that darken round the wave-worn rover
Rang his clarion higher than winds cried round the ship,
Rose a pageant of set suns and storms blown over,
Hands that held life's guerdons fast or let them slip.
But no tongue may tell, no thanksgiving discover,
Half the heaven of blessing, soft with clouds that drip,
Keen with beams that kindle, dear as love to lover,
Opening by the spell's strength on his lyric lip.

XVI.

By that spell the soul transfigured and dilated
Puts forth wings that widen, breathes a brightening air,
Feeds on light and drinks of music, whence elated
All her sense grows godlike, seeing all depths made bare,
All the mists wherein before she sat belated
Shrink, till now the sunlight knows not if they were;
All this earth transformed is Eden recreated,
With the breath of heaven remurmuring in her hair.

XVII.

Sweeter far than aught of sweet that April nurses
Deep in dew-dropt woodland folded fast and furled
Breathes the fragrant song whose burning dawn disperses
Darkness, like the surge of armies backward hurled,
Even as though the touch of spring's own hand, that pierces
Earth with life's delight, had hidden in the impearled
Golden bells and buds and petals of his verses
All the breath of all the flowers in all the world.

XVIII.

But the soul therein, the light that our souls follow,
Fires and fills the song with more of prophet's pride,
More of life than all the gulfs of death may swallow,
More of flame than all the might of night may hide.
Though the whole dark age were loud and void and hollow,
Strength of trust were here, and help for all souls tried,
And a token from the flight of that strange swallow6
Whose migration still is toward the wintry side.

XIX.

Never came such token for divine solution
From the oraculous live darkness whence of yore
Ancient faith sought word of help and retribution,
Truth to lighten doubt, a sign to go before.
Never so baptismal waters of ablution
Bathed the brows of exile on so stern a shore,
Where the lightnings of the sea of revolution
Flashed across them ere its thunders yet might roar.

XX.

By the lightning's light of present revelation
Shown, with epic thunder as from skies that frown,
Clothed in darkness as of darkling expiation,
Rose a vision of dead stars and suns gone down,
Whence of old fierce fire devoured the star-struck nation,
Till its wrath and woe lit red the raging town,
Now made glorious with his statue's crowning station,
Where may never gleam again a viler crown.

XXI.

King, with time for throne and all the years for pages,
He shall reign though all thrones else be over-hurled,
Served of souls that have his living words for wages,
Crowned of heaven each dawn that leaves his brows impearled;
Girt about with robes unrent of storm that rages,
Robes not wrought with hands, from no loom's weft unfurled;
All the praise of all earth's tongues in all earth's ages,
All the love of all men's hearts in all the world.

XXII.

Yet what hand shall carve the soul or cast the spirit,
Mould the face of fame, bid glory's feature glow?
Who bequeath for eyes of ages hence to inherit
Him, the Master, whom love knows not if it know?
Scarcely perfect praise of men man's work might merit,
Scarcely bid such aim to perfect stature grow,
Were his hand the hand of Phidias who shall rear it,
And his soul the very soul of Angelo.

XXIII.

Michael, awful angel of the world's last session,
Once on earth, like him, with fire of suffering tried,
Thine it were, if man's it were, without transgression,
Thine alone, to take this toil upon thy pride.
Thine, whose heart was great against the world's oppression,
Even as his whose word is lamp and staff and guide:
Advocate for man, untired of intercession,
Pleads his voice for slaves whose lords his voice defied.

XXIV.

Earth, with all the kings and thralls on earth, below it,
Heaven alone, with all the worlds in heaven, above,
Let his likeness rise for suns and stars to know it,
High for men to worship, plain for men to love:
Brow that braved the tides which fain would overflow it,
Lip that gave the challenge, hand that flung the glove;
Comforter and prophet, Paraclete and poet,
Soul whose emblems are an eagle and a dove.

XXV.

Sun, that hast not seen a loftier head wax hoary,
Earth, which hast not shown the sun a nobler birth,
Time, that hast not on thy scroll denied and gory
One man's name writ brighter in its whole wide girth,
Witness, till the final years fulfil their story,
Till the stars break off the music of their mirth,
What among the sons of men was this man's glory,
What the vesture of his soul revealed on earth.

SONNETS

HOPE AND FEAR

Beneath the shadow of dawn's aerial cope,
With eyes enkindled as the sun's own sphere,
Hope from the front of youth in godlike cheer
Looks Godward, past the shades where blind men grope
Round the dark door that prayers nor dreams can ope,
And makes for joy the very darkness dear
That gives her wide wings play; nor dreams that fear
At noon may rise and pierce the heart of hope.
Then, when the soul leaves off to dream and yearn,

May truth first purge her eyesight to discern
What once being known leaves time no power to appal;
Till youth at last, ere yet youth be not, learn
The kind wise word that falls from years that fall—
'Hope thou not much, and fear thon not at all.'

AFTER SUNSET

'Si quis piorum Manibus locus.'

I.

Straight from the sun's grave in the deep clear west
A sweet strong wind blows, glad of life: and I,
Under the soft keen stardawn whence the sky
Takes life renewed, and all night's godlike breast
Palpitates, gradually revealed at rest
By growth and change of ardours felt on high,
Make onward, till the last flame fall and die
And all the world by night's broad hand lie blest.
Haply, meseems, as from that edge of death,
Whereon the day lies dark, a brightening breath
Blows more of benediction than the morn,
So from the graves whereon grief gazing saith
That half our heart of life there lies forlorn
May light or breath at least of hope be born.

II.

The wind was soft before the sunset fled:
Now, while the cloud-enshrouded corpse of day
Is lowered along a red funereal way
Down to the dark that knows not white from red,
A clear sheer breeze against the night makes head,
Serene, but sure of life as ere a ray
Springs, or the dusk of dawn knows red from grey,
Being as a soul that knows not quick from dead.
From far beyond the sunset, far above,
Full toward the starry soundless east it blows
Bright as a child's breath breathing on a rose,
Smooth to the sense as plume of any dove;
Till more and more as darkness grows and glows
Silence and night seem likest life and love.

III.

If light of life outlive the set of sun
That men call death and end of all things, then
How should not that which life held best for men
And proved most precious, though it seem undone
By force of death and woful victory won,
Be first and surest of revival, when
Death shall bow down to life arisen again?
So shall the soul seen be the self-same one
That looked and spake with even such lips and eyes
As love shall doubt not then to recognise,
And all bright thoughts and smiles of all time past
Revive, transfigured, but in spirit and sense
None other than we knew, for evidence
That love's last mortal word was not his last

A STUDY FROM MEMORY

If that he yet a living soul which here
Seemed brighter for the growth of numbered springs
And clothed by Time and Pain with goodlier things
Each year it saw fulfilled a fresh fleet year,
Death can have changed not aught that made it dear;
Half humorous goodness, grave-eyed mirth on wings
Bright-balanced, blither-voiced than quiring strings;
Most radiant patience, crowned with conquering cheer;
A spirit inviolable that smiled and sang
By might of nature and heroic need
More sweet and strong than loftiest dream or deed;
A song that shone, a light whence music rang
High as the sunniest heights of kindliest thought;
All these must be, or all she was be nought

TO DR. JOHN BROWN

Beyond the north wind lay the land of old
Where men dwelt blithe and blameless, clothed and fed
With joy's bright raiment and with love's sweet bread,
The whitest flock of earth's maternal fold.
None there might wear about his brows enrolled
A light of lovelier fame than rings your head,
Whose lovesome love of children and the dead
All men give thanks for: I far off behold

A dear dead hand that links us, and a light
The blithest and benignest of the night,
The night of death's sweet sleep, wherein may be
A star to show your spirit in present sight
Some happier island in the Elysian sea
Where Rab may lick the hand of Marjorie.

March 1882

TO WILLIAM BELL SCOTT

The larks are loud above our leagues of whin
Now the sun's perfume fills their glorious gold
With odour like the colour: all the wold
Is only light and song and wind wherein
These twain are blent in one with shining din.
And now your gift, a giver's kingly-souled,
Dear old fast friend whose honours grow not old,
Bids memory's note as loud and sweet begin.
Though all but we from life be now gone forth
Of that bright household in our joyous north
Where I, scarce clear of boyhood just at end,
First met your hand; yet under life's clear dome,
Now seventy strenuous years have crowned my friend,
Shines no less bright his full-sheaved harvest-home.

April 20, 1882

A DEATH ON EASTER DAY

The strong spring sun rejoicingly may rise,
Rise and make revel, as of old men said,
Like dancing hearts of lovers newly wed:
A light more bright than ever bathed the skies
Departs for all time out of all men's eyes.
The crowns that girt last night a living head
Shine only now, though deathless, on the dead:
Art that mocks death, and Song that never dies.
Albeit the bright sweet mothlike wings be furled,
Hope sees, past all division and defection,
And higher than swims the mist of human breath,
The soul most radiant once in all the world
Requickened to regenerate resurrection
Out of the likeness of the shadow of death.

April 1883,

ON THE DEATHS OF THOMAS CARLYLE AND GEORGE ELIOT

Two souls diverse out of our human sight
Pass, followed one with love and each with wonder:
The stormy sophist with his mouth of thunder,
Clothed with loud words and mantled in the might
Of darkness and magnificence of night;
And one whose eye could smite the night in sunder,
Searching if light or no light were thereunder,
And found in love of loving-kindness light.
Duty divine and Thought with eyes of fire
Still following Righteousness with deep desire
Shone sole and stern before her and above,
Sure stars and sole to steer by; but more sweet
Shone lower the loveliest lamp for earthly feet,
The light of little children, and their love.

AFTER LOOKING INTO CARLYLES REMINISCENCES

I.

Three men lived yet when this dead man was young
Whose names and words endure for ever one:
Whose eyes grew dim with straining toward the sun,
And his wings weakened, and his angel's tongue
Lost half the sweetest song was ever sung,
But like the strain half uttered earth hears none,
Nor shall man hear till all men's songs are done:
One whose clear spirit like an eagle hung
Between the mountains hallowed by his love
And the sky stainless as his soul above:
And one the sweetest heart that ever spake
The brightest words wherein sweet wisdom smiled.
These deathless names by this dead snake denied
Bid memory spit upon him for their sake.

II.

Sweet heart, forgive me for thine own sweet sake,
Whose kind blithe soul such seas of sorrow swam,

And for my love's sake, powerless as I am
For love to praise thee, or like thee to make
Music of mirth where hearts less pure would break,
Less pure than thine, our life-unspotted Lamb.
Things hatefullest thou hadst not heart to damn,
Nor wouldst have set thine heel on this dead snake.
Let worms consume its memory with its tongue,
The fang that stabbed fair Truth, the lip that stung
Men's memories uncorroded with its breath.
Forgive me, that with bitter words like his
I mix the gentlest English name that is,
The tenderest held of all that know not death.

A LAST LOOK

Sick of self-love, Malvolio, like an owl
That hoots the sun rerisen where starlight sank,
With German garters crossed athwart thy frank
Stout Scottish legs, men watched thee snarl and scowl,
And boys responsive with reverberate howl
Shrilled, hearing how to thee the springtime stank
And as thine own soul all the world smelt rank
And as thine own thoughts Liberty seemed foul.
Now, for all ill thoughts nursed and ill words given
Not all condemned, not utterly forgiven,
Son of the storm and darkness, pass in peace.
Peace upon earth thou knewest not: now, being dead,
Rest, with nor curse nor blessing on thine head,
Where high-strung hate and strenuous envy cease.

DICKENS

Chief in thy generation born of men
Whom English praise acclaimed as English-born,
With eyes that matched the worldwide eyes of morn
For gleam of tears or laughter, tenderest then
When thoughts of children warmed their light, or when
Reverence of age with love and labour worn,
Or godlike pity fired with godlike scorn,
Shot through them flame that winged thy swift live pen:
Where stars and suns that we behold not burn,
Higher even than here, though highest was here thy place,
Love sees thy spirit laugh and speak and shine
With Shakespeare and the soft bright soul of Sterne

And Fielding's kindliest might and Goldsmith's grace
Scarce one more loved or worthier love than thine.

ON LAMB'S SPECIMENS OF DRAMATIC POETS

I.

If all the flowers of all the fields on earth
By wonder-working summer were made one,
Its fragrance were not sweeter in the sun,
Its treasure-house of leaves were not more worth
Than those wherefrom thy light of musing mirth
Shone, till each leaf whereon thy pen would run
Breathed life, and all its breath was benison.
Beloved beyond all names of English birth,
More dear than mightier memories; gentlest name
That ever clothed itself with flower-sweet fame,
Or linked itself with loftiest names of old
By right and might of loving; I, that am
Less than the least of those within thy fold,
Give only thanks for them to thee, Charles Lamb.

II.

So many a year had borne its own bright bees
And slain them since thy honey-bees were hived,
John Day, in cells of flower-sweet verse contrived
So well with craft of moulding melodies,
Thy soul perchance in amaranth fields at ease
Thought not to hear the sound on earth revived
Of summer music from the spring derived
When thy song sucked the flower of flowering trees
But thine was not the chance of every day:
Time, after many a darkling hour, grew sunny,
And light between the clouds ere sunset swam,
Laughing, and kissed their darkness all away,
When, touched and tasted and approved, thy honey
Took subtler sweetness from the lips of Lamb.

TO JOHN NICHOL

I.

Friend of the dead, and friend of all my days
Even since they cast off boyhood, I salute
The song saluting friends whose songs are mute
With full burnt-offerings of clear-spirited praise.
That since our old young years our several ways
Have led through fields diverse of flower and fruit
Yet no cross wind has once relaxed the root
We set long since beneath the sundawn's rays,
The root of trust whence towered the trusty tree,
Friendship this only and duly might impel
My song to salutation of your own;
More even than praise of one unseen of me
And loved the starry spirit of Dobell,
To mine by light and music only known.

II.

But more than this what moves me most of all
To leave not all unworded and unsped
The whole heart's greeting of my thanks unsaid
Scarce needs this sign, that from my tongue should fall
His name whom sorrow and reverent love recall,
The sign to friends on earth of that dear head
Alive, which now long since untimely dead
The wan grey waters covered for a pall.
Their trustless reaches dense with tangling stems
Took never life more taintless of rebuke,
More pure and perfect, more serene and kind,
Than when those clear eyes closed beneath the Thames,
And made the now more hallowed name of Luke
Memorial to us of morning left behind.

May 1881.

DYSTHANATOS

Ad generem Cereris sine cæde et vulnere pauci
Descendunt reges, aut siccâ morte tyranni.

By no dry death another king goes down
The way of kings. Yet may no free man's voice,
For stern compassion and deep awe, rejoice
That one sign more is given against the crown,
That one more head those dark red waters drown
Which rise round thrones whose trembling equipoise

Is propped on sand and bloodshed and such toys
As human hearts that shrink at human frown.
The name writ red on Polish earth, the star
That was to outshine our England's in the far
East heaven of empire where is one that saith
Proud words now, prophesying of this White Czar?
'In bloodless pangs few kings yield up their breath,
Few tyrants perish by no violent death,'

March 14, 1881.

EUONYMOS

εὖ μὴν ᾗ τιμὴν ἐδέδου νικηφόρος ἀλκὴ
ἐκ νίκης ὄνομ' ἔσχε φόβου κέαρ αἰὲν ἄθικτος.

A year ago red wrath and keen despair
Spake, and the sole word from their darkness sent
Laid low the lord not all omnipotent
Who stood most like a god of all that were
As gods for pride of power, till fire and air
Made earth of all his godhead. Lightning rent
The heart of empire's lurid firmament,
And laid the mortal core of manhood bare.
But when the calm crowned head that all revere
For valour higher than that which casts out fear,
Since fear came near it never, comes near death,
Blind murder cowers before it, knowing that here
No braver soul drew bright and queenly breath
Since England wept upon Elizabeth.

March 8, 1882.

ON THE RUSSIAN PERSECUTION OF THE JEWS

O son of man, by lying tongues adored,
By slaughterous hands of slaves with feet red-shod
In carnage deep as ever Christian trod
Profaned with prayer and sacrifice abhorred
And incense from the trembling tyrant's horde,
Brute worshippers or wielders of the rod,
Most murderous even of all that call thee God,
Most treacherous even that ever called thee Lord;
Face loved of little children long ago,

Head hated of the priests and rulers then,
If thou see this, or hear these hounds of thine
Run ravening as the Gadarean swine,
Say, was not this thy Passion, to foreknow
In death's worst hour the works of Christian men?

Jan. 23, 1882.

BISMARCK AT CANOSSA

Not all disgraced, in that Italian town,
The imperial German cowered beneath thine hand,
Alone indeed imperial Hildebrand,
And felt thy foot and Rome's, and felt her frown
And thine, more strong and sovereign than his crown,
Though iron forged its blood-encrusted band.
But now the princely wielder of his land,
For hatred's sake toward freedom, so bows down,
No strength is in the foot to spurn: its tread
Can bruise not now the proud submitted head:
But how much more abased, much lower brought low,
And more intolerably humiliated,
The neck submissive of the prosperous foe,
Than his whom scorn saw shuddering in the snow!

December 31, 1881.

QUIA NOMINOR LEO

I.

What part is left thee, lion? Ravenous beast,
Which hadst the world for pasture, and for scope
And compass of thine homicidal hope
The kingdom of the spirit of man, the feast
Of souls subdued from west to sunless east,
From blackening north to bloodred south aslope,
All servile; earth for footcloth of the pope,
And heaven for chancel-ceiling of the priest;
Thou that hadst earth by right of rack and rod,
Thou that hadst Rome because thy name was God,
And by thy creed's gift heaven wherein to dwell;
Heaven laughs with all his light and might above
That earth has cast thee out of faith and love;

Thy part is but the hollow dream of hell.

II.

The light of life has faded from thy cause,
High priest of heaven and hell and purgatory:
Thy lips are loud with strains of oldworld story,
But the red prey was rent out of thy paws
Long since and they that dying brake down thy laws
Have with the fires of death-enkindled glory
Put out the flame that faltered on thy hoary
High altars, waning with the world's applause.
This Italy was Dante's Bruno died
Here Campanella, too sublime for pride,
Endured thy God's worst here, and hence went home.
And what art thou, that time's full tide should shrink
For thy sake downward? What art thou, to think
Thy God shall give thee back for birthright Rome?

January, 1882.

THE CHANNEL TUNNEL

Not for less love, all glorious France, to thee,
'Sweet enemy' called in days long since at end.
Now found and hailed of England sweeter friend,
Bright sister of our freedom now, being free;
Not for less love or faith in friendship we
Whose love burnt ever toward thee reprehend
The vile vain greed whose pursy dreams portend
Between our shores suppression of the sea.
Not by dull toil of blind mechanic art
Shall these be linked for no man's force to part
Nor length of years and changes to divide,
But union only of trust and loving heart
And perfect faith in freedom strong to abide
And spirit at one with spirit on either side.

April 3, 1881.

SIR WILLIAM GOMM

I.

At three score years and five aroused anew
To rule in India, forth a soldier went
On whose bright-fronted youth fierce war had spent
Its iron stress of storm, till glory grew
Full as the red sun waned on Waterloo.
Landing, he met the word from England sent
Which bade him yield up rule: and he, content,
Resigned it, as a mightier warrior's due;
And wrote as one rejoicing to record
That 'from the first' his royal heart was lord
Of its own pride or pain; that thought was none
Therein save this, that in her perilous strait
England, whose womb brings forth her sons so great,
Should choose to serve her first her mightiest son.

II.

Glory beyond all flight of warlike fame
Go with the warrior's memory who preferred
To praise of men whereby men's hearts are stirred,
And acclamation of his own proud name
With blare of trumpet-blasts and sound and flame
Of pageant honour, and the titular word
That only wins men worship of the herd,
His country's sovereign good: who overcame
Pride, wrath, and hope of all high chance on earth,
For this land's love that gave his great heart birth.
O nursling of the sea-winds and the sea,
Immortal England, goddess ocean-born,
What shall thy children fear, what strengths not scorn,
While children of such mould are born to thee?

EUTHANATOS

In Memory of Mrs. Thellusson

Forth of our ways and woes,
Forth of the winds and snows,
A white soul soaring goes,
Winged like a dove:
So sweet, so pure, so clear,
So heavenly tempered here,
Love need not hope or fear her changed above:
Ere dawned her day to die,

So heavenly, that on high
Change could not glorify
Nor death refine her:
Pure gold of perfect love,
On earth like heaven's own dove,
She cannot wear, above, a smile diviner.

Her voice in heaven's own quire
Can sound no heavenlier lyre
Than here no purer fire
Her soul can soar:
No sweeter stars her eyes
In unimagined skies
Beyond our sight can rise than here before,

Hardly long years had shed
Their shadows on her head:
Hardly we think her dead,
Who hardly thought her
Old: hardly can believe
The grief our hearts receive
And wonder while they grieve, as wrong were wrought her.

But though strong grief be strong
No word or thought of wrong
May stain the trembling song,
Wring the bruised heart,
That sounds or sighs its faint
Low note of love, nor taint
Grief for so sweet a saint, when such depart.

A saint whose perfect soul,
With perfect love for goal,
Faith hardly might control,
Creeds might not harden:
A flower more splendid far
Than the most radiant star
Seen here of all that are in God's own garden.

Surely the stars we see
Rise and relapse as we,
And change and set, may be
But shadows too:
But spirits that man's lot
Could neither mar nor spot
Like these false lights are not, being heavenly true.

Not like these dying lights

Of worlds whose glory smites
The passage of the nights
Through heaven's blind prison:
Not like their souls who see,
If thought fly far and free,
No heavenlier heaven to be for souls rerisen.

A soul wherein love shone
Even like the sun, alone,
With fervour of its own
And splendour fed,
Made by no creeds less kind
Toward souls by none confined,
Could Death's self quench or blind, Love's self were dead.

February 4, 1881.

FIRST AND LAST

Upon the borderlands of being,
Where life draws hardly breath
Between the lights and shadows fleeing
Fast as a word one saith,
Two flowers rejoice our eyesight, seeing
The dawns of birth and death.
Behind the babe his dawn is lying
Half risen with notes of mirth
From all the winds about it flying
Through new-born heaven and earth:
Before bright age his day for dying
Dawns equal-eyed with birth.

Equal the dews of even and dawn,
Equal the sun's eye seen
A hand's breadth risen and half withdrawn
But no bright hour between
Brings aught so bright by stream or lawn
To noonday growths of green.

Which flower of life may smell the sweeter
To love's insensual sense,
Which fragrance move with offering meeter
His soothed omnipotence,
Being chosen as fairer or as fleeter,
Borne hither or borne hence,

Love's foiled omniscience knows not: this
Were more than all he knows
With all his lore of bale and bliss,
The choice of rose and rose,
One red as lips that touch with his,
One white as moonlit snows.

No hope is half so sweet and good,
No dream of saint or sage
So fair as these are: no dark mood
But these might best assuage;
The sweet red rose of babyhood,
The white sweet rose of age,

LINES ON THE DEATH OF EDWARD JOHN TRELAWNY

Last high star of the years whose thunder
Still men's listening remembrance hears,
Last light left of our fathers' years,
Watched with honour and hailed with wonder
Thee too then have the years borne under,
Thou too then hast regained thy peers.
Wings that warred with the winds of morning,
Storm-winds rocking the red great dawn,
Close at last, and a film is drawn
Over the eyes of the storm-bird, scorning
Now no longer the loud wind's warning,
Waves that threaten or waves that fawn.

Peers were none of thee left us living,
Peers of theirs we shall see no more.
Eight years over the full fourscore
Knew thee: now shalt thou sleep, forgiving
All griefs past of the wild world's giving,
Moored at last on the stormless shore.

Worldwide liberty's lifelong lover,
Lover no less of the strength of song,
Sea-king, swordsman, hater of wrong,
Over thy dust that the dust shall cover
Comes my song as a bird to hover,
Borne of its will as of wings along.

Cherished of thee were this brief song's brothers
Now that follows them, cherishing thee.
Over the tides and the tideless sea

Soft as a smile of the earth our mother's
Flies it faster than all those others,
First of the troop at thy tomb to be.

Memories of Greece and the mountain's hollow
Guarded alone of thy loyal sword
Hold thy name for our hearts in ward:
Yet more fain are our hearts to follow
One way now with the southward swallow
Back to the grave of the man their lord.

Heart of hearts, art thou moved not, hearing
Surely, if hearts of the dead may hear,
Whose true heart it is now draws near?
Surely the sense of it thrills thee, cheering
Darkness and death with the news now nearing
Shelley, Trelawny rejoins thee here.

ADIEUX À MARIE STUART

I.

Queen, for whose house my fathers fought,
With hopes that rose and fell,
Red star of boyhood's fiery thought,
Farewell

They gave their lives, and I, my queen,
Have given you of my life,
Seeing your brave star burn high between
Men's strife.

The strife that lightened round their spears
Long since fell still: so long
Hardly may hope to last in years
My song.

But still through strife of time and thought
Your light on me too fell:
Queen, in whose name we sang or fought,
Farewell.

II.

There beats no heart on either border

Wherethrough the north blasts blow
But keeps your memory as a warder
His beacon-fire aglow.

Long since it fired with love and wonder
Mine, for whose April age
Blithe midsummer made banquet under
The shade of Hermitage.

Soft sang the burn's blithe notes, that gather
Strength to ring true:
And air and trees and sun and heather
Remembered you.

Old border ghosts of fight or fairy
Or love or teen,
These they forgot, remembering Mary
The Queen.

III.

Queen once of Scots and ever of ours
Whose sires brought forth for you
Their lives to strew your way like flowers,
Adieu.

Dead is full many a dead man's name
Who died for you this long
Time past: shall this too fare the same,
My song?

But surely, though it die or live,
Your face was worth
All that a man may think to give
On earth.

No darkness cast of years between
Can darken you:
Man's love will never bid my queen
Adieu.

IV.

Love hangs like light about your name
As music round the shell:
No heart can take of you a tame

Farewell.

Yet, when your very face was seen,
Ill gifts were yours for giving:
Love gat strange guerdons of my queen
When living.

O diamond heart unflawed and clear,
The whole world's crowning jewel!
Was ever heart so deadly dear
So cruel?

Yet none for you of all that bled
Grudged once one drop that fell:
Not one to life reluctant said
Farewell

V.

Strange love they have given you, love disloyal,
Who mock with praise your name,
To leave a head so rare and royal
Too low for praise or blame.

You could not love nor hate, they tell us,
You had nor sense nor sting:
In God's name, then, what plague befell us
To fight for such a thing?

'Some faults the gods will give' to fetter
Man's highest intent:
But surely you were something better
Than innocent!

No maid that strays with steps unwary
Through snares unseen,
But one to live and die for; Mary,
The Queen.

VI.

Forgive them all their praise, who blot
Your fame with praise of you:
Then love may say, and falter not
Adieu.

Yet some you hardly would forgive
Who did you much less wrong
Once: but resentment should not live
Too long.

They never saw your lip's bright bow,
Your swordbright eyes,
The bluest of heavenly things below
The skies.

Clear eyes that love's self finds most like
A swordblade's blue,
A swordblade's ever keen to strike,
Adieu.

VII.

Though all things breathe or sound of fight
That yet make up your spell,
To bid you were to bid the light
Farewell

Farewell the song says only, being
A star whose race is run:
Farewell the soul says never, seeing
The sun.

Yet, wellnigh as with flash of tears,
The song must say but so
That took your praise up twenty years
Ago,

More bright than stars or moons that vary,
Sun kindling heaven and hell,
Here, after all these years, Queen Mary,
Farewell

HERSE

When grace is given us ever to behold
A child some sweet months old,
Love, laying across our lips his finger, saith,
Smiling, with bated breath,
Hush! for the holiest thing that lives is here,
And heaven's own heart how near!

How dare we, that may gaze not on the sun,
Gaze on this verier one?
Heart, hold thy peace; eyes, be cast down for shame;
Lips, breathe not yet its name.
In heaven they know what name to call it; we,
How should we know? For, see!
The adorable sweet living marvellous
Strange light that lightens us
Who gaze, desertless of such glorious grace,
Full in a babe's warm face!
All roses that the morning rears are nought,
All stars not worth a thought,
Set this one star against them, or suppose
As rival this one rose.
What price could pay with earth's whole weight of geld
One least flushed roseleafs fold
Of all this dimpling store of smiles that shine
From each warm curve and line,
Each charm of flower-sweet flesh, to reillume
The dappled rose-red bloom
Of all its dainty body, honey-sweet
Clenched hands and curled-up feet,
That on the roses of the dawn have trod
As they came down from God,
And keep the flush and colour that the sky
Takes when the sun comes nigh,
And keep the likeness of the smile their grace
Evoked on God's own face
When, seeing this work of his most heavenly mood,
He saw that it was good?
For all its warm sweet body seems one smile,
And mere men's love too vile
To meet it, or with eyes that worship dims
Read o'er the little limbs,
Read all the book of all their beauties o'er,
Rejoice, revere, adore,
Bow down and worship each delight in turn,
Laugh, wonder, yield, and yearn.
But when our trembling kisses dare, yet dread,
Even to draw nigh its head,
And touch, and scarce with touch or breath surprise
Its mild miraculous eyes
Out of their viewless vision—O, what then,
What may be said of men?
What speech may name a new-born child? what word
Earth ever spake or heard?
The best men's tongue that ever glory knew
Called that a drop of dew

Which from the breathing creature's kindly womb
Came forth in blameless bloom.
We have no word, as had those men most high,
To call a baby by.
Rose, ruby, lily, pearl of stormless seas—
A better word than these,
A better sign it was than flower or gem
That love revealed to them:
They knew that whence comes light or quickening flame,
Thence only this thing came,
And only might be likened of our love
To somewhat born above,
Not even to sweetest things dropped else on earth,
Only to dew's own birth.
Nor doubt we but their sense was heavenly true,
Babe, when we gaze on you,
A dew-drop out of heaven whose colours are
More bright than sun or star,
As now, ere watching love dare fear or hope,
Lips, hands, and eyelids ope,
And all your life is mixed with earthly leaven.
O child, what news from heaven?

TWINS

Affectionately Inscribed to W.M.R. and L.R.

April, on whose wings
Ride all gracious things,
Like the star that brings
All things good to man,
Ere his light, that yet
Makes the month shine, set,
And fair May forget
Whence her birth began,
Brings, as heart would choose,
Sound of golden news,
Bright as kindling dews
When the dawn begins;
Tidings clear as mirth,
Sweet as air and earth
Now that hail the birth,
Twice thus blest, of twins.

In the lovely land
Where with hand in hand

Lovers wedded stand
Other joys before
Made your mixed life sweet:
Now, as Time sees meet,
Three glad blossoms greet
Two glad blossoms more.

Fed with sun and dew,
While your joys were new,
First arose and grew
One bright olive-shoot:
Then a fair and fine
Slip of warm-haired pine
Felt the sweet sun shine
On its leaf and fruit,

And it wore for mark
Graven on the dark
Beauty of its bark
That the noblest name
Worn in song of old
By the king whose bold
Hand had fast in hold
All the flower of fame.

Then, with southern skies
Flattered in her eyes,
Which, in lovelier wise
Yet, reflect their blue
Brightened more, being bright
Here with life's delight,
And with love's live light
Glorified anew,

Came, as fair as came
One who bore her name
(She that broke as flame
From the swan-shell white),
Crowned with tender hair
Only, but more fair
Than all queens that were
Themes of oldworld fight,

Of your flowers the third
Bud, or new-fledged bird
In your hearts' nest heard
Murmuring like a dove
Bright as those that drew

Over waves where blew
No loud wind the blue
Heaven-hued car of love.

Not the glorious grace
Even of that one face
Potent to displace
All the towers of Troy
Surely shone more clear
Once with childlike cheer
Than this child's face here
Now with living joy.

After these again
Here in April's train
Breaks the bloom of twain
Blossoms in one birth
For a crown of May
On the front of day
When he takes his way
Over heaven and earth.

Half a heavenly thing
Given from heaven to Spring
By the sun her king,
Half a tender toy,
Seems a child of curl
Yet too soft to twirl;
Seems the flower-sweet girl
By the flower-bright boy.

All the kind gods' grace,
All their love, embrace
Ever either face,
Ever brood above them:
All soft wings of hours
Screen them as with flowers
From all beams and showers:
All life's seasons love them.

When the dews of sleep
Falling lightliest keep
Eyes too close to peep
Forth and laugh off rest,
Joy from face to feet
Fill them, as is meet;
Life to them be sweet
As their mother's breast

When those dews are dry,
And in day's bright eye
Looking full they lie
Bright as rose and pearl,
All returns of joy
Pure of time's alloy
Bless the rose-red boy,
Guard the rose-white girl.

POSTSCRIPT

Friends, if I could take
Half a note from Blake
Or but one verse make
Of the Conqueror's mine,
Better than my best
Song above your nest
I would sing: the quest
Now seems too divine.

April 28, 1881.

THE SALT OF THE EARTH

If childhood were not in the world,
But only men and women grown;
No baby-locks in tendrils curled,
No baby-blossoms blown;
Though men were stronger, women fairer,
And nearer all delights in reach,
And verse and music uttered rarer
Tones of more godlike speech;

Though the utmost life of life's best hours
Found, as it cannot now find, words;
Though desert sands were sweet as flowers
And flowers could sing like birds,

But children never heard them, never
They felt a child's foot leap and run:
This were a drearier star than ever
Yet looked upon the sun.

SEVEN YEARS OLD

I.

Seven white roses on one tree,
Seven white loaves of blameless leaven,
Seven white sails on one soft sea,
Seven white swans on one lake's lee,
Seven white flowerlike stars in heaven,
All are types unmeet to be
For a birthday's crown of seven.

II.

Not the radiance of the roses,
Not the blessing of the bread,
Not the breeze that ere day grows is
Fresh for sails and swans, and closes
Wings above the sun's grave spread,
When the starshine on the snows is
Sweet as sleep on sorrow shed,

III.

Nothing sweetest, nothing best,
Holds so good and sweet a treasure
As the love wherewith once blest
Joy grows holy, grief takes rest,
Life, half tired with hours to measure,
Fills his eyes and lips and breast
With most light and breath of pleasure

IV.

As the rapture unpolluted,
As the passion undefiled,
By whose force all pains heart-rooted
Are transfigured and transmuted,
Recompensed and reconciled,
Through the imperial, undisputed,
Present godhead of a child.

V.

Brown bright eyes and fair bright head,
Worth a worthier crown than this is,
Worth a worthier song instead,
Sweet grave wise round mouth, full fed
With the joy of love, whose bliss is
More than mortal wine and bread,
Lips whose words are sweet as kisses,

VI.

Little hands so glad of giving,
Little heart so glad of love,
Little soul so glad of living,
While the strong swift hours are weaving
Light with darkness woven above,
Time for mirth and time for grieving,
Plume of raven and plume of dove,

VII.

I can give you but a word
Warm with love therein for leaven,
But a song that falls unheard
Yet on ears of sense unstirred
Yet by song so far from heaven,
Whence you came the brightest bird,
Seven years since, of seven times seven.

EIGHT YEARS OLD

I.

Sun, whom the faltering snow-cloud fears,
Rise, let the time of year be May,
Speak now the word that April hears,
Let March have all his royal way;
Bid all spring raise in winter's ears
All tunes her children hear or play,
Because the crown of eight glad years
On one bright head is set to-day.

II.

What matters cloud or sun to-day
To him who wears the wreath of years
So many, and all like flowers at play
With wind and sunshine, while his ears
Hear only song on every way?
More sweet than spring triumphant hears
Ring through the revel-rout of May
Are these, the notes that winter fears.

III.

Strong-hearted winter knows and fears
The music made of love at play,
Or haply loves the tune he hears
From hearts fulfilled with flowering May,
Whose molten music thaws his ears
Late frozen, deaf but yesterday
To sounds of dying and dawning years,
Now quickened on his deathward way.

IV.

For deathward now lies winter's way
Down the green vestibule of years
That each year brightens day by day
With flower and shower till hope scarce fears
And fear grows wholly hope of May.
But we—the music in our ears
Made of love's pulses as they play
The heart alone that makes it hears.

V.

The heart it is that plays and hears
High salutation of to-day.
Tongue falters, hand shrinks back, song fears
Its own unworthiness to play
Fit music for those eight sweet years,
Or sing their blithe accomplished way.
No song quite worth a young child's ears
Broke ever even from birds in May.

VI.

There beats not in the heart of May,
When summer hopes and springtide fears,
There falls not from the height of day,
When sunlight speaks and silence hears,
So sweet a psalm as children play
And sing, each hour of all their years,
Each moment of their lovely way,
And know not how it thrills our ears.

VII.

Ah child, what are we, that our ears
Should hear you singing on your way,
Should have this happiness? The years
Whose hurrying wings about us play
Are not like yours, whose flower-time fears
Nought worse than sunlit showers in May,
Being sinless as the spring, that hears
Her own heart praise her every day.

VIII.

Yet we too triumph in the day
That bare, to entrance our eyes and ears,
To lighten daylight, and to play
Such notes as darkness knows and fears,
The child whose face illumes our way,
Whose voice lifts up the heart that hears,
Whose hand is as the hand of May
To bring us flowers from eight full years.

February 4, 1882.

COMPARISONS

Child, when they say that others
Have been or are like you,
Babes fit to be your brothers,
Sweet human drops of dew,
Bright fruit of mortal mothers,
What should one say or do?
We know the thought is treason,
We feel the dream absurd;

A claim rebuked of reason,
That withers at a word:
For never shone the season
That bore so blithe a bird.

Some smiles may seem as merry,
Some glances gleam as wise,
From lips as like a cherry
And scarce less gracious eyes;
Eyes browner than a berry,
Lips red as morning's rise.
But never yet rang laughter
So sweet in gladdened ears
Through wall and floor and rafter
As all this household hears
And rings response thereafter
Till cloudiest weather clears.

When those your chosen of all men,
Whose honey never cloys,
Two lights whose smiles enthrall men,
Were called at your age boys,
Those mighty men, while small men,
Could make no merrier noise.

Our Shakespeare, surely, daffed not
More lightly pain aside
From radiant lips that quaffed not
Of forethought's tragic tide:
Our Dickens, doubtless, laughed not
More loud with life's first pride.

The dawn were not more cheerless
With neither light nor dew
Than we without the fearless
Clear laugh that thrills us through:
If ever child stood peerless,
Love knows that child is you

WHAT IS DEATH!

Looking on a page where stood
Graven of old on old-world wood
Death, and by the grave's edge grim,
Pale, the young man facing him,
Asked my well-beloved of me

Once what strange thing this might be,
Gaunt and great of limb.
Death, I told him: and, surprise
Deepening more his wildwood eyes
(Like some sweet fleet thing's whose breath
Speaks all spring though nought it saith),
Up he turned his rosebright face
Glorious with its seven years' grace,
Asking—What is death?

A CHILD'S PITY

No sweeter thing than children's ways and wiles,
Surely, we say, can gladden eyes and ears:
Yet sometime sweeter than their words or smiles
Are even their tears.
To one for once a piteous tale was read,
How, when the murderous mother crocodile
Was slain, her fierce brood famished, and lay dead,
Starved, by the Nile.

In vast green reed-beds on the vast grey slime
Those monsters motherless and helpless lay,
Perishing only for the parent's crime
Whose seed were they.

Hours after, toward the dusk, our blithe small bird
Of Paradise, who has our hearts in keeping,
Was heard or seen, but hardly seen or heard,
For pity weeping.

He was so sorry, sitting still apart,
For the poor little crocodiles, he said.
Six years had given him, for an angel's heart,
A child's instead.

Feigned tears the false beasts shed for murderous ends,
We know from travellers' tales of crocodiles:
But these tears wept upon them of my friend's
Outshine his smiles.

What heavenliest angels of what heavenly city
Could match the heavenly heart in children here?
The heart that hallowing all things with its pity
Casts out all fear?

So lovely, so divine, so dear their laughter
Seems to us, we know not what could be more dear:
But lovelier yet we see the sign thereafter
Of such a tear.

With sense of love half laughing and half weeping
We met your tears, our small sweet-spirited friend:
Let your love have us in its heavenly keeping
To life's last end.

A CHILD'S LAUGHTER

All the bells of heaven may ring,
All the birds of heaven may sing,
All the wells on earth may spring,
All the winds on earth may bring
All sweet sounds together;
Sweeter far than all things heard,
Hand of harper, tone of bird,
Sound of woods at sundawn stirred,
Welling water's winsome word,
Wind in warm wan weather,
One thing yet there is, that none
Hearing ere its chime be done
Knows not well the sweetest one
Heard of man beneath the sun,
Hoped in heaven hereafter;
Soft and strong and loud and light,
Very sound of very light
Heard from morning's rosiest height,
When the soul of all delight
Fills a child's clear laughter.

Golden bells of welcome rolled
Never forth such notes, nor told
Hours so blithe in tones so bold,
As the radiant mouth of gold
Here that rings forth heaven.
If the golden-crested wren
Were a nightingale—why, then,
Something seen and heard of men
Might be half as sweet as when
Laughs a child of seven.

A CHILD'S THANKS

How low soe'er men rank us,
How high soe'er we win,
The children far above us
Dwell, and they deign to love us,
With lovelier love than ours,
And smiles more sweet than flowers;
As though the sun should thank us
For letting light come in.
With too divine complaisance,
Whose grace misleads them thus,
Being gods, in heavenly blindness
They call our worship kindness,
Our pebble-gift a gem:
They think us good to them,
Whose glance, whose breath, whose presence,
Are gifts too good for us.

The poet high and hoary
Of meres that mountains bind
Felt his great heart more often
Yearn, and its proud strength soften
From stern to tenderer mood,
At thought of gratitude
Shown than of song or story
He heard of hearts unkind.

But with what words for token
And what adoring tears
Of reverence risen to passion,
In what glad prostrate fashion
Of spirit and soul subdued,
May man show gratitude
For thanks of children spoken
That hover in his ears?

The angels laugh, your brothers,
Child, hearing you thank me,
With eyes whence night grows sunny,
And touch of lips like honey,
And words like honey-dew:
But how shall I thank you?
For gifts above all others
What guerdon-gift may be?

What wealth of words caressing,
What choice of songs found best,

Would seem not as derision,
Found vain beside the vision
And glory from above
Shown in a child's heart's love?
His part in life is blessing;
Ours, only to be blest.

A CHILD'S BATTLES

πὺξ ἀρετὰν εὑρών—PINDAR.

Praise of the knights of old
May sleep: their tale is told,
And no man cares:
The praise which fires our lips is
A knight's whose fame eclipses
All of theirs.
The ruddiest light in heaven
Blazed as his birth-star seven
Long years ago·
All glory crown that old year
Which brought our stout small soldier
With the snow!

Each baby born has one
Star, for his friends a sun,
The first of stars:
And we, the more we scan it,
The more grow sure your planet,
Child, was Mars.

For each one flower, perchance,
Blooms as his cognizance:
The snowdrop chill,
The violet unbeholden,
For some: for you the golden
Daffodil

Erect, a fighting flower,
It breasts the breeziest hour
That ever blew,
And bent or broke things brittle
Or frail, unlike a little
Knight like you

Its flower is firm and fresh

And stout like sturdiest flesh
Of children: all
The strenuous blast that parches
Spring hurts it not till March is
Near his fall

If winds that prate and fret
Remark, rebuke, regret,
Lament, or blame
The brave plant's martial passion,
It keeps its own free fashion
All the same.

We that would fain seem wise
Assume grave mouths and eyes
Whose looks reprove
Too much delight in battle:
But your great heart our prattle
Cannot move.

We say, small children should
Be placid, mildly good
And blandly meek:
Whereat the broad smile rushes
Full on your lips, and flushes
All your cheek.

If all the stars that are
Laughed out, and every star
Could here be heard,
Such peals of golden laughter
We should not hear, as after
Such a word.

For all the storm saith, still,
Stout stands the daffodil:
For all we say,
Howe'er he look demurely,
Our martialist will surely
Have his way.

We may not bind with bands
Those large and liberal hands,
Nor stay from fight,
Nor hold them back from giving
No lean mean laws of living
Bind a knight

And always here of old
Such gentle hearts and bold
Our land has bred:
How durst her eye rest else on
The glory shed from Nelson
Quick and dead?

Shame were it, if but one
Such once were born her son,
That one to have borne,
And brought him ne'er a brother:
His praise should bring his mother
Shame and scorn.

A child high-souled as he
Whose manhood shook the sea
Smiles haply here:
His face, where love lies basking,
With bright shut mouth seems asking,
What is fear?

The sunshine-coloured fists
Beyond his dimpling wrists
Were never closed
For saving or for sparing—
For only deeds of daring
Predisposed

Unclenched, the gracious hands
Let slip their gifts like sands
Made rich with ore
That tongues of beggars ravish
From small stout hands so lavish
Of their store.

Sweet hardy kindly hands
Like these were his that stands
With heel on gorge
Seen trampling down the dragon
On sign or flask or flagon,
Sweet Saint George.

Some tournament, perchance,
Of hands that couch no lance,
Might mark this spot
Your lists, if here some pleasant
Small Guenevere were present,
Launcelot.

My brave bright flower, you need
No foolish song, nor heed
It more than spring
The sighs of winter stricken
Dead when your haunts requicken
Here, my king.

Yet O, how hardly may
The wheels of singing stay
That whirl along
Bright paths whence echo raises
The phantom of your praises,
Child, my song!

Beyond all other things
That give my words fleet wings,
Fleet wings and strong,
You set their jesses ringing
Till hardly can I, singing,
Stint my song.

But all things better, friend,
And worse must find an end:
And, right or wrong,
'Tis time, lest rhyme should baffle,
I doubt, to put a snaffle
On my song.

And never may your ear
Aught harsher hear or fear,
Nor wolfish night
Nor dog-toothed winter snarling
Behind your steps, my darling
My delight!

For all the gifts you give
Me, dear, each day you live,
Of thanks above
All thanks that could be spoken
Take not my song in token,
Take my love.

A CHILD'S FUTURE

What will it please you, my darling, hereafter to be?

Fame upon land will you look for, or glory by sea?
Gallant your life will be always, and all of it free.
Free as the wind when the heart of the twilight is stirred
Eastward, and sounds from the springs of the sunrise are heard:
Free—and we know not another as infinite word.

Darkness or twilight or sunlight may compass us round,
Hate may arise up against us, or hope may confound;
Love may forsake us; yet may not the spirit be bound.

Free in oppression of grief as in ardour of joy
Still may the soul be, and each to her strength as a toy:
Free in the glance of the man as the smile of the boy.

Freedom alone is the salt and the spirit that gives
Life, and without her is nothing that verily lives:
Death cannot slay her: she laughs upon death and forgives.

Brightest and hardiest of roses anear and afar
Glitters the blithe little face of you, round as a star:
Liberty bless you and keep you to be as you are.

England and liberty bless you and keep you to be
Worthy the name of their child and the sight of their sea:
Fear not at all; for a slave, if he fears not, is free.

SONNETS ON ENGLISH DRAMATIC POETS (1590-1650):

I.

CHRISTOPHER MARLOWE

Crowned, girdled, garbed and shod with light and fire,
Son first-born of the morning, sovereign star!
Soul nearest ours of all, that wert most far,
Most far off in the abysm of time, thy lyre
Hung highest above the dawn-enkindled quire
Where all ye sang together, all that are,
And all the starry songs behind thy car
Rang sequence, all our souls acclaim thee sire.
'If all the pens that ever poets held
Had fed the feeling of their masters' thoughts,'
And as with rush of hurtling chariots
The flight of all their spirits were impelled
Toward one great end, thy glory—nay, not then,
Not yet might'st thou be praised enough of men.

II

WILLIAM SHAKESPEARE

Not if men's tongues and angels' all in one
Spake, might the word be said that might speak Thee,
Streams, winds, woods, flowers, fields, mountains, yea, the sea,
What power is in them all to praise the sun?
His praise is this, he can be praised of none.
Man, woman, child, praise God for him; but he
Exults not to be worshipped, but to be.
He is; and, being, beholds his work well done.
All joy, all glory, all sorrow, all strength, all mirth,
Are his: without him, day were night on earth.
Time knows not his from time's own period.
All lutes, all harps, all viols, all flutes, all lyres,
Fall dumb before him ere one string suspires.
All stars are angels; but the sun is God.

III.

BEN JONSON

Broad-based, broad-fronted, bounteous, multiform,
With many a valley impleached with ivy and vine,
Wherein the springs of all the streams run wine,
And many a crag full-faced against the storm,
The mountain where thy Muse's feet made warm
Those lawns that revelled with her dance divine
Shines yet with fire as it was wont to shine
From tossing torches round the dance aswarm.
Nor less, high-stationed on the grey grave heights,
High-thoughted seers with heaven's heart-kindling lights
Hold converse: and the herd of meaner things
Knows or by fiery scourge or fiery shaft
When wrath on thy broad brows has risen, and laughed,
Darkening thy soul with shadow of thunderous wings.

IV

BEAUMONT AND FLETCHER

An hour ere sudden sunset fired the west,
Arose two stars upon the pale deep east.
The hall of heaven was clear for night's high feast,
Yet was not yet day's fiery heart at rest
Love leapt up from his mother's burning breast
To see those warm twin lights, as day decreased,
Wax wider, till when all the sun had ceased
As suns they shone from evening's kindled crest
Across them and between, a quickening fire,
Flamed Venus, laughing with appeased desire.
Their dawn, scarce lovelier for the gleam of tears,
Filled half the hollow shell 'twixt heaven and earth
With sound like moonlight, mingling moan and mirth,
Which rings and glitters down the darkling years.

V.

PHILIP MASSINGER

Clouds here and there arisen an hour past noon
Chequered our English heaven with lengthening bars
And shadow and sound of wheel-winged thunder-cars
Assembling strength to put forth tempest soon,
When the clear still warm concord of thy tune
Rose under skies unscared by reddening Mars
Yet, like a sound of silver speech of stars,
With full mild flame as of the mellowing moon.
Grave and great-hearted Massinger, thy face
High melancholy lights with loftier grace
Than gilds the brows of revel: sad and wise,
The spirit of thought that moved thy deeper song,
Sorrow serene in soft calm scorn of wrong,
Speaks patience yet from thy majestic eyes.

VI.

JOHN FORD

Hew hard the marble from the mountain's heart
Where hardest night holds fast in iron gloom
Gems brighter than an April dawn in bloom,
That his Memnoniah likeness thence may start
Revealed, whose hand with high funereal art

Carved night, and chiselled shadow: be the tomb
That speaks him famous graven with signs of doom
Intrenched inevitably in lines athwart,
As on some thunder-blasted Titan's brow
His record of rebellion. Not the day
Shall strike forth music from so stern a chord,
Touching this marble: darkness, none knows how,
And stars impenetrable of midnight, may.
So looms the likeness of thy soul, John Ford.

VII.

JOHN WEBSTER

Thunder: the flesh quails, and the soul bows down.
Night: east, west, south, and northward, very night
Star upon struggling star strives into sight,
Star after shuddering star the deep storms drown.
The very throne of night, her very crown,
A man lays hand on, and usurps her right
Song from the highest of heaven's imperious height
Shoots, as a fire to smite some towering town.
Rage, anguish, harrowing fear, heart-crazing crime,
Make monstrous all the murderous face of Time
Shown in the spheral orbit of a glass
Revolving. Earth cries out from all her graves.
Frail, on frail rafts, across wide-wallowing waves,
Shapes here and there of child and mother pass.

VIII.

THOMAS DEKKER

Out of the depths of darkling life where sin
Laughs piteously that sorrow should not know
Her own ill name, nor woe be counted woe;
Where hate and craft and lust make drearier din
Than sounds through dreams that grief holds revel in;
What charm of joy-bells ringing, streams that flow,
Winds that blow healing in each note they blow,
Is this that the outer darkness hears begin?
O sweetest heart of all thy time save one,
Star seen for love's sake nearest to the sun,
Hung lamplike o'er a dense and doleful city,

Not Shakespeare's very spirit, howe'er more great,
Than thine toward man was more compassionate,
Nor gave Christ praise from lips more sweet with pity.

IX.

THOMAS MIDDLETON

A wild moon riding high from cloud to cloud,
That sees and sees not, glimmering far beneath,
Hell's children revel along the shuddering heath
With dirge-like mirth and raiment like a shroud:
A worse fair face than witchcraft's, passion-proud,
With brows blood-flecked behind their bridal wreath
And lips that bade the assassin's sword find sheath
Deep in the heart whereto love's heart was vowed:
A game of close contentious crafts and creeds
Played till white England bring black Spain to shame:
A son's bright sword and brighter soul, whose deeds
High conscience lights for mother's love and fame:
Pure gipsy flowers, and poisonous courtly weeds:
Such tokens and such trophies crown thy name.

X.

THOMAS HEYWOOD

Tom, if they loved thee best who called thee Tom.
What else may all men call thee, seeing thus bright
Even yet the laughing and the weeping light
That still thy kind old eyes are kindled from?
Small care was thine to assail and overcome
Time and his child Oblivion: yet of right
Thy name has part with names of lordlier might
For English love and homely sense of home,
Whose fragrance keeps thy small sweet bayleaf young
And gives it place aloft among thy peers
Whence many a wreath once higher strong Time has hurled:
And this thy praise is sweet on Shakespeare's tongue—
'O good old man, how well in thee appears
The constant service of the antique world!'

XI.

GEORGE CHAPMAN

High priest of Homer, not elect in vain,
Deep trumpets blow before thee, shawms behind
Mix music with the rolling wheels that wind
Slow through the labouring triumph of thy train:
Fierce history, molten in thy forging brain,
Takes form and fire and fashion from thy mind,
Tormented and transmuted out of kind:
But howsoe'er thou shift thy strenuous strain,
Like Tailor smooth, like Fisher swollen, and now
Grim Yarrington scarce bloodier marked than thou,
Then bluff as Mayne's or broad-mouthed Barry's glee,
Proud still with hoar predominance of brow
And beard like foam swept off the broad blown sea,
Where'er thou go, men's reverence goes with thee.

XII.

JOHN MARSTON

The bitterness of death and bitterer scorn
Breathes from the broad-leafed aloe-plant whence thou
Wast fain to gather for thy bended brow
A chaplet by no gentler forehead worn.
Grief deep as hell, wrath hardly to be borne,
Ploughed up thy soul till round the furrowing plough
The strange black soil foamed, as a black beaked prow
Bids night-black waves foam where its track has torn.
Too faint the phrase for thee that only saith
Scorn bitterer than the bitterness of death
Pervades the sullen splendour of thy soul,
Where hate and pain make war on force and fraud
And all the strengths of tyrants; whence unflawed
It keeps this noble heart of hatred whole.

XIII.

JOHN DAY

Day was a full-blown flower in heaven, alive
With murmuring joy of bees and birds aswarm,

When in the skies of song yet flushed and warm
With music where all passion seems to strive
For utterance, all things bright and fierce to drive
Struggling along the splendour of the storm,
Day for an hour put off his fiery form,
And golden murmurs from a golden hive
Across the strong bright summer wind were heard,
And laughter soft as smiles from girls at play
And loud from lips of boys brow-bound with May.
Our mightiest age let fall its gentlest word,
When Song, in semblance of a sweet small bird,
Lit fluttering on the light swift hand of Day.

XIV.

JAMES SHIRLEY

The dusk of day's decline was hard on dark
When evening trembled round thy glowworm lamp
That shone across her shades and dewy damp
A small clear beacon whose benignant spark
Was gracious yet for loiterers' eyes to mark,
Though changed the watchword of our English camp
Since the outposts rang round Marlowe's lion ramp,
When thy steed's pace went ambling round Hyde Park.
And in the thickening twilight under thee
Walks Davenant, pensive in the paths where he,
The blithest throat that ever carolled love
In music made of morning's merriest heart,
Glad Suckling, stumbled from his seat above
And reeled on slippery roads of alien art.

XV.

THE TRIBE OF BENJAMIN

Sons born of many a loyal Muse to Ben,
All true-begotten, warm with wine or ale,
Bright from the broad light of his presence, hail!
Prince Randolph, nighest his throne of all his men,
Being highest in spirit and heart who hailed him then
King, nor might other spread so blithe a sail:
Cartwright, a soul pent in with narrower pale,
Praised of thy sire for manful might of pen:

Marmion, whose verse keeps alway keen and fine
The perfume of their Apollonian wine
Who shared with that stout sire of all and thee
The exuberant chalice of his echoing shrine:
Is not your praise writ broad in gold which he
Inscribed, that all who praise his name should see?

XVI.

ANONYMOUS PLAYS:

'ARDEN OF FEVERSHAM'

Mother whose womb brought forth our man of men,
Mother of Shakespeare, whom all time acclaims
Queen therefore, sovereign queen of English dames,
Throned higher than sat thy sonless empress then,
Was it thy son's young passion-guided pen
Which drew, reflected from encircling flames,
A figure marked by the earlier of thy names
Wife, and from all her wedded kinswomen
Marked by the sign of murderess? Pale and great,
Great in her grief and sin, but in her death
And anguish of her penitential breath
Greater than all her sin or sin-born fate,
She stands, the holocaust of dark desire,
Clothed round with song for ever as with fire.

XVII.

ANONYMOUS PLAYS

Ye too, dim watchfires of some darkling hour,
Whose fame forlorn time saves not nor proclaims
For ever, but forgetfulness defames
And darkness and the shadow of death devour,
Lift up ye too your light, put forth your power,
Let the far twilight feel your soft small flames
And smile, albeit night name not even their names,
Ghost by ghost passing, flower blown down on flower:
That sweet-tongued shadow, like a star's that passed
Singing, and light was from its darkness cast
To paint the face of Painting fair with praise:[1]
And that wherein forefigured smiles the pure

Fraternal face of Wordsworth's Elidure
Between two child-faced masks of merrier days.[2]

[1.] *Doctor Dodypol*
[2.] *Nobody and Somebody*

XVIII.

ANONYMOUS PLAYS

More yet and more, and yet we mark not all:
The Warning fain to bid fair women heed
Its hard brief note of deadly doom and deed;[1]
The verse that strewed too thick with flowers the hall
Whence Nero watched his fiery festival;[2]
That iron page wherein men's eyes who read
See, bruised and marred between two babes that bleed,
A mad red-handed husband's martyr fall;[3]
The scene which crossed and streaked with mirth the strife
Of Henry with his sons and witchlike wife;[4]
And that sweet pageant of the kindly fiend,
Who, seeing three friends in spirit and heart made one,
Crowned with good hap the true-love wiles he screened
In the pleached lanes of pleasant Edmonton.[5]

[1.] *A Warning for Fair Women.*
[2.] *The Tragedy of Nero.*
[3.] *A Yorkshire Tragedy.*
[4.] *Look about you.*
[5.] *The Merry Devil o Edmonton.*

XIX.

THE MANY

Greene, garlanded with February's few flowers,
Ere March came in with Marlowe's rapturous rage:
Peele, from whose hand the sweet white locks of age
Took the mild chaplet woven of honoured hours:
Nash, laughing hard: Lodge, flushed from lyric bowers:
And Lilly, a goldfinch in a twisted cage
Fed by some gay great lady's pettish page
Till short sweet songs gush clear like short spring showers
Kid, whose grim sport still gambolled over graves:

And Chettle, in whose fresh funereal verse
Weeps Marian yet on Robin's wildwood hearse:
Cooke, whose light boat of song one soft breath saves,
Sighed from a maiden's amorous mouth averse:
Live likewise ye: Time takes not you for slaves.

II.

Haughton, whose mirth gave woman all her will:
Field, bright and loud with laughing flower and bird
And keen alternate notes of laud and gird:
Barnes, darkening once with Borgia's deeds the quill
Which tuned the passion of Parthenophil:
Blithe burly Porter, broad and bold of word:
Wilkins, a voice with strenuous pity stirred:
Turk Mason: Brewer, whose tongue drops honey still
Rough Rowley, handling song with Esau's hand:
Light Nabbes: lean Sharpham, rank and raw by turns,
But fragrant with a forethought once of Burns:
Soft Davenport, sad-robed, but blithe and bland:
Brome, gipsy-led across the woodland ferns:
Praise be with all, and place among our band.

XXI.

EPILOGUE

Our mother, which wast twice, as history saith,
Found first among the nations: once, when she
Who bore thine ensign saw the God in thee
Smite Spain, and bring forth Shakespeare: once, when death
Shrank, and Rome's bloodhounds cowered, at Milton's breath:
More than thy place, then first among the free,
More than that sovereign lordship of the sea
Bequeathed to Cromwell from Elizabeth,
More than thy fiery guiding- star, which Drake
Hailed, and the deep saw lit again for Blake,
More than all deeds wrought of thy strong right hand,
This praise keeps most thy fame's memorial strong,
That thou wast head of all these streams of song,
And time bows down to thee as Shakespeare's land.

Algernon Charles Swinburne – A Short Biography

Algernon Charles Swinburne was born at 7 Chester Street, Grosvenor Place, in London, on April 5th, 1837. He was the eldest of six children born to Captain Charles Henry Swinburne and Lady Jane Henrietta, daughter of the 3rd Earl of Ashburnham, a wealthy Northumbrian family.

Swinburne spent his early years at East Dene in Bonchurch, on the Isle of Wight. As a child, Swinburne was nervous and frail, but also imbued with a nervous energy and fearlessness almost to the point of recklessness.

He was schooled at Eton College from 1849 to 1853. It was here that he first began to write poetry. He excelled at languages and whilst still at Eton won first prizes in both French and Italian.

From Eton he moved to Oxford where he attended at Balliol College from 1856. Here he met friends to whom he became closely attached, among them Dante Gabriel Rossetti, William Morris and Edward Burne-Jones, who in 1857, were painting their Arthurian murals on the walls of the Oxford Union. At Oxford Swinburne was mentored by Benjamin Jowett, the master of Balliol College, who recognised his poetic talent and, intervening on his behalf, tried to keep him from being expelled when he celebrated the Italian patriot Orsini, and his failed attempt on the life of Napoleon III in 1858. Swinburne had to leave the Universcity for a few months due to this but returned in May, 1860 but never received a degree.

Summers were usually spent at Capheaton Hall in Northumberland, the house of his grandfather, Sir John Swinburne, 6th Baronet, who had a famous library and was himself President of the Literary and Philosophical Society in Newcastle upon Tyne.

Swinburne proudly considered himself a native of Northumberland and this is reflected in poems such as the intensely patriotic 'Northumberland' and 'Grace Darling'. He enjoyed riding across the moors and was, it was said, a daring horseman, as he moved 'through honeyed leagues of the northland border', as he remembered the Scottish border in his Recollections.

In the period from 1857 to 1860, Swinburne was one of a number of Pre-Raphaelite's who visited and became part of Lady Pauline Trevelyan's intellectual circle at Wallington Hall, a few miles west of Morpeth in Northumberland.

After leaving college, he moved to London and began his career in earnest as well as becoming a constant visitor to the Rossetti's house. To Rossetti Swinburne was his 'little Northumbrian friend', an affectionate reference to Swinburne's small stature—a mere five foot four. Whatever Swinburne lacked in height he made up for in poetic talent. However, with the burden of such great talent came the unveiling of a dark side that was to cause him pain and would, at times, threaten his very existence with all manner of self-inflicted pains through drink, drugs and sado-machoism.

In 1860 Swinburne published two verse dramas; The Queen Mother and Rosamond but it would not be until 1865 that Swinburne would achieve literary success with Atalanta in Calydon.

In 1861, Swinburne visited Menton on the French Riviera to recover from the effects of yet another period of excess use of alcohol, staying at the Villa Laurenti. From Menton, Swinburne then travelled on to Italy, where he journeyed widely.

After Elizabeth Rossetti's death from suicide in 1862, he and Rossetti moved to Tudor House at 16 Cheyne Walk in Chelsea. The stories that survive from his year with Rossetti are typical Swinburne. In one, Rossetti once had to tell him to keep down the noise — he and a boyfriend had been sliding naked down the bannisters and disturbing Rossetti's painting. He took a sardonic delight in what the critic and biographer, Cecil Lang, calls "Algernonic exaggeration": When people began to talk scathingly about his homosexuality and other sexual proclivities, he circulated a story that he had engaged in pederasty and bestiality with a monkey — and then eaten it. How many of the stories were true and how many invented is unclear. Oscar Wilde called him "a braggart in matters of vice, who had done everything he could to convince his fellow citizens of his homosexuality and bestiality without being in the slightest degree a homosexual or a bestialiser."

In December 1862, Swinburne accompanied Scott and his guests on a trip to Tynemouth. Scott writes in his memoirs that, as they walked by the sea, Swinburne declaimed the as yet unpublished 'Hymn to Proserpine' and 'Laus Veneris' in his lilting intonation, while the waves 'were running the whole length of the long level sands towards Cullercoats and sounding like far-off acclamations'.

Swinburne possessed a curious combination of frail health and strength. He was small and slightly built, but an excellent swimmer and the first to climb Culver Cliff on the Isle of Wight. He had an extremely excitable disposition: people who met him described him as a "demoniac boy" who would go skipping about the room declaiming poetry at the top of his voice. In this as in many things, moderation was not the standard for him. Excess was. Once or twice he had fits, thought to be epileptic, in public; but he made this condition much worse by drinking past excess to unconsciousness. More than once he was delivered to the door in the small of the night, dead drunk. Throughout the 1860s and '70s he rode an alcoholic cycle of dissolution, collapse, drying out at home in the country, then returning to London where he would begin the cycle all over again.

His mania for masochism, particularly flagellation, most probably started in early childhood at Eton and was encouraged by his later friendships with Richard Monckton Milnes (one of Tennyson's fellow Apostles), who introduced him to the works of the Marquis de Sade, and Richard Burton, the Victorian explorer and adventurer. Swinburne was an alcoholic and algolagniac (a desire for sexual gratification through inflicting pain on oneself or others; sadomasochism). He found life difficult, unfulfilling but still his poetic talents pushed to the fore.

Although Swinburne continued to publish some works in periodicals in 1865 he was granted recognition by both public and critics with Atalanta in Calydon written in the style of a classical Greek tragedy.

There followed "Laus Veneris" and Poems and Ballads (1866), with their sexually charged passages, absolutely decadent for polite Victorian society, which were attacked all the more violently as a result. The poems written in homage of Sappho of Lesbos such as "Anactoria" and "Sapphics" were especially savaged. The volume also contained poems such as "The Leper," "Laus Veneris," and "St Dorothy" which evoke both Swinburne's and a general Victorian fascination with the Middle Ages, and are explicitly mediaeval in style, tone and construction. With its publication came instant notoriety. He was now identified with indecent and decadent themes and the precept of art for art's sake.

Swinburne's meeting in 1867 with his long-time hero Mazzini, the Italian patriot living in England in exile, was the beginning of a poetical journey that now became more serious and more engaged with serious thought, initially leading to the political poems in the volume Songs Before Sunrise.

Also in 1867 he was introduced to Adah Isaacs Menken, the American actress, poet and circus rider, whose main fame seemed to be riding naked on a horse (in fact she wore tight nude coloured clothing) for her performance in the melodrama Mazeppa (itself based on a poem by Lord Byron). Although they had a short affair Adah's quote implies that Swinburne was not ready for a relationship that did not involve some self-sabotage; "I can't make him understand that biting's no use."

In 1879, with Swinburne nearly dead from alcoholism and dissolution, his legal advisor Theodore Watts-Dunton took him in, and was gradually successful in getting him to adapt to a healthier lifestyle. Swinburne lived the rest of his life at Watts-Dunton's house. He saw less and less of his old bohemian friends, who thought him a prisoner at The Pines, but his growing deafness also accounts for some of his decreased sociability. By now Swinburne was 42, and was moving from a young man of rebelliousness to a figure of social respectability. It was said of Watts-Dunton that he saved the man and killed the poet.

It is clear that Swinburne had an addictive personality, and clearly incapable of moderation in his pursuit of any chosen vices. This, of course, would both nourish and perhaps sabotage his poetic career. His poetry follows the somewhat clichéd pattern of early flourish and later decline; indeed some of the fresher pieces in the second and third series of Poems and Ballads (published in 1878 and 1889) were actually written during his days at Oxford. Nevertheless, his last collection, A Channel Passage, has some beautiful poems, including "The Lake of Gaube."

He is best remembered as the supreme technician in metre, with a versatility which exceeds even Tennyson's, but which lacks a corresponding emotional range. His obsessions are not widely enough shared; and if he cannot shock us by the strangeness of his desires nor the shrillness of his anti-theistical exclamations, often what remains is not enough to fully engage with the audience.

Swinburne is considered a poet of the decadent school, although he perhaps professed to more vice than he actually indulged in to advertise his deviance. Common gossip of the time reported that he also had a deep crush on the explorer Sir Richard Francis Burton, despite the fact that Swinburne himself abhorred travel. Fact and fiction are easily absorbed by the other so are difficult to untangle even now.

Many critics consider his mastery of vocabulary, rhyme and metre impressive, although he has also been criticised for his florid style and word choices that only fit the rhyme scheme rather than contributing to the meaning of the piece. A. E. Housman, although a critic, had great praise for his rhyming ability: to Swinburne the sonnet was child's play: the task of providing four rhymes was not hard enough, and he wrote long poems in which each stanza required eight or ten rhymes, and wrote them so that he never seemed to be saying anything for the rhyme's sake.

Throughout his career Swinburne published literary criticism of great worth. His deep knowledge of world literatures contributed to a critical style rich in quotation, allusion, and comparison. He is particularly noted for discerning studies of Elizabethan dramatists and of many English and French poets and novelists. As well he was a noted essayist and wrote two novels.

Swinburne was nominated for the Nobel Prize in Literature every year from 1903 to 1907 and then again in 1909.

H.P. Lovecraft, the master of the dark side and a decent poet himself, considered Swinburne "the only real poet in either England or America after the death of Mr. Edgar Allan Poe."

Swinburne was also responsible for devising a poetic form called the roundel, a variation of the French Rondeau form. In 1883 he published A Century of Roundels with several of the roundels dedicated to Dante's sister, the poet Christina Georgina Rossetti. Swinburne wrote to Edward Burne-Jones in 1883: "I have got a tiny new book of songs or songlets, in one form and all manner of metres ... just coming out, of which Miss Rossetti has accepted the dedication. I hope you and Georgie [his wife Georgiana] will find something to like among a hundred poems of nine lines each, twenty-four of which are about babies or small children".

Opinions of the Roundel poems move between those who find them captivating and brilliant, to others who find them merely clever and contrived. One of them, A Baby's Death, was set to music by the English composer Sir Edward Elgar as the song "Roundel: The little eyes that never knew Light".

After the first Poems and Ballads, Swinburne's later poetry was devoted more to philosophy and politics, including the unification of Italy, particularly in the volume Songs before Sunrise. He did not stop writing love poetry entirely, indeed it was only in 1882 that his great epic-length poem, Tristram of Lyonesse, was published, its contents lyrical rather than shocking. His versification, and especially his rhyming technique, remain of high quality to the end.

Algernon Charles Swinburne died of influenza, at the Pines in London on April 10th, 1909 at the age of 72. He was buried at St. Boniface Church, Bonchurch on the Isle of Wight.

Algernon Charles Swinburne – A Concise Bibliography

Verse Drama
The Queen Mother (1860)
Rosamond (1860)
Chastelard (1865)
Bothwell (1874)
Mary Stuart (1881)
Marino Faliero (1885)
Locrine (1887)
The Sisters (1892)
Rosamund, Queen of the Lombards (1899)

Poetry
Atalanta in Calydon (1865)*
Poems and Ballads (1866)
Songs Before Sunrise (1871)
Songs of Two Nations (1875)
Erechtheus (1876)*
Poems and Ballads, Second Series (1878)
Songs of the Springtides (1880)
Studies in Song (1880)
The Heptalogia, or the Seven against Sense. A Cap with Seven Bells (1880)
Tristram of Lyonesse (1882)
A Dark Month & Other Poems

A Century of Roundels (1883)
A Midsummer Holiday and Other Poems (1884)
Poems and Ballads, Third Series (1889)
Astrophel and Other Poems (1894)
The Tale of Balen (1896)
A Channel Passage and Other Poems (1904)

*Although formally tragedies, Atlanta in Calydon and Erechtheus are traditionally included with his poetry.

Criticism

William Blake: A Critical Essay (1868, new edition 1906)
Under the Microscope (1872)
George Chapman: A Critical Essay (1875)
Essays and Studies (1875)
A Note on Charlotte Brontë (1877)
A Study of Shakespeare (1880)
A Study of Victor Hugo (1886)
A Study of Ben Johnson (1889)
Studies in Prose and Poetry (1894)
The Age of Shakespeare (1908)
Shakespeare (1909)

Major Collections

The Poems of Algernon Charles Swinburne, 6 vols. 1904.
The Tragedies of Algernon Charles Swinburne, 5 vols. 1905.
The Complete Works of Algernon Charles Swinburne, 20 vols. Bonchurch Edition. 1925-7.
The Swinburne Letters, 6 vols. 1959-62.

www.ingramcontent.com/pod-product-compliance
Lightning Source LLC
Chambersburg PA
CBHW060136050426
42448CB00010B/2160